I'VE GOT THE MISSION STATEMENT, NOW WHAT?

8 Core Competencies for Transformational Leadership

KATHRYN NERMOE

Latitude 13 LLC

I've got the mission statement, now what? is available for sale at Amazon.com
in print, Kindle and audio versions.

Grateful acknowledgement is made to Rich Winter and the Todd County
Tribune for permission to reprint a March 14, 2013 article entitled
"Rosebud Sioux Tribe Diabetes Prevention breaks ground for Wellness
Center," by Rich Winter.

ISBN-10: 1492158461
ISBN-13: 9781492158462

Cover Design by Kevin Tobosa

Author Photo by Lisa Johansen

*This book is dedicated to all
of the men and women in the
United States Armed Forces who fight
for our citizenship every day.*

TABLE OF CONTENTS

FORWARD

The United Way made a significant shift over a decade ago. That shift stemmed from the age-old lesson - *Money alone doesn't buy happiness.* At least what the United Way was beginning to realize, in today's society, donations alone do not create sustaining change in communities.

Yes, non-profit organizations need financial stability in order to fulfill their missions. The United Way has helped community-based organizations meet this financial need for over a century. But more so, we have found when financial contributions are combined with an engagement strategy, the return on investment is tenfold.

Non-profit groups and government alike need the talent and hearts of corporate employees to help solve some of our nation's most pressing challenges. Conversely, many of our corporate employees are experiencing and have fallen victim to those very challenges that non-profits and government are addressing in the first place. We are all interconnected, and we all have skin in the game. The United Way's engagement strategy with the private sector is an example of how collectively and authentically bringing community into the workplace, or by letting the workplace be a part of the community, social problems have a greater chance of being solved.

Today's new United Way has become a leading agent for creating this necessary problem-solving synergy across all sectors. In addition to building financial capacity for communities, the United Way is equally focused on building human capacity. Time and time again, United Way communities experiencing the highest degree of positive change are those with the strongest support of community CEOs, executives and organizational leaders. People are influenced most by those in leadership positions. And people are most efficiently mobilized where their primary sense of membership resides – their workplace.

Engaging corporations beyond money isn't easy. It means asking a high-tech company, as demonstrated by 3M, to apply its employees' wealth of innovation and ideation to social issues; to volunteer in their community to tutor and mentor young girls, specifically with a STEM (Science, Technology, Engineering, Mathematics) focus; and then give them scholarships to attend college to become the next 3M innovator.

I've got the mission statement, now what? reveals *why* engaging corporations beyond money isn't easy. It's because the majority of Americans aren't fully engaged in the workplace. This is where our hard work as leaders begins...

This book builds upon the United Way's call for engagement across the nation by asking executives to consider how building social capital is equally beneficial for business *and* community. It asks organizational leaders to view human capital through a new lens – as citizens.

High social capital creates higher functioning systems – whether its community, business, government, or the economy. *I've got the mission statement, now what?* offers practical steps for any leader to create a win-win by building social capital inside and outside the walls of their organization.

Laura Bowman, The United Way
Laura Bowman has spent her entire career with the United Way. She is the President of the United Way of Olmsted County (Rochester, MN), former President of the Greater Mankato Area United Way (Mankato, MN), and former Vice President of the Sioux Empire United Way (Sioux Falls, SD).

PREFACE

An executive I once worked with kicked off our team meetings with what she called the word game. This is where we went around the room, and using just one word, needed to capture how we felt about the day, the last week, or perhaps it was about a major project we had just completed.

If today's average corporate employee was asked to participate in this word game, describing with just one word how they feel, I think the word most often used would be *tired*. Tired of corporate games and politics. Tired of the new 60-hour work weeks. Tired of not feeling appreciated and valued for their contributions to the organization.

The Ripple Effect

When employees are feeling tired, the ripple effect into both our corporations and communities is unfortunate, resulting in reduced productivity and diminished citizenry. *I've got the mission statement, now what?* presents a new set of core competencies for a new generation of leadership. It offers eight steps for organizational leaders to reignite engagement in both corporation and community.

Throughout my career, I've heard countless stories with too many common themes. We've all exhibited frustration because we feel our work lacks purpose; felt guilty for not spending enough time with family or missing our kids' activities; skipped a vacation because we felt we couldn't get away from work; or last, worked while we were supposed to be on vacation. Many Americans have forgotten what it means to shut the cell phone off and be on vacation (even more are laughing at the sheer proposal that you would even consider doing such a thing).

Most concerning, I've noticed a growing trend with professionals who are now underemployed for the main purpose of achieving the quality of life they are looking for; because they tried, and found they cannot achieve their definition of success at home *and* work at the same time.

Today's lack of loyalty between people and organizations doesn't allow families to put their roots down the way they once did and become embedded in their communities. An increasing number of people live their lives with a Plan B ready for activation in their back pocket - where they know they can pick up and move if they need to at a moment's notice. They feel little ownership and responsibility to the community they live in. After all, it might be temporary...

A New Lens for Leaders

Corporate leaders should feel direct ownership for the lives of the people who serve their corporate cause; but somehow that has gotten lost and it's time to rebuild social capital both inside and outside the walls of our organizations. Robert Putnam's (Harvard University Kennedy School of Government) research surrounding the decline of citizen engagement is presented in this book against the backdrop of today's decline in employee engagement. I do not think this correlation is simply a coincidence. *I've got the mission statement, now what?* offers a new perspective on how closely they are tied together. When we successfully engage our workforce, not only does it improve operational performance and profitability, it translates into an engaged society. Collectively, the net effect is a stronger economy.

Whether we're at home or at work, research reveals we aren't at our best and this has taken its toll on our nation. My career path has been somewhat unique in that I've held leadership positions in all three sectors - public, private and nonprofit. I've seen firsthand a common and pervasive thread woven between all three: The need for engagement - employee engagement, citizen engagement and donor engagement. All three sectors are facing the same problem and our leaders are the solution.

This book is designed as a handbook to guide organizational leaders in seeing human capital through a new lens - to see their workplaces as communities and their employees as citizens. It's a consolidation of ideas, research and a new perspective that serves as a roadmap for citizen-centered leadership. Most organizations today have the intellectual know-how to be successful. What they lack is an appreciation surrounding the principles of engagement and how building social capital creates a corporate competitive advantage. Organizations with high social capital solve problems more quickly, they are more efficient, and in the end, are more profitable.

If after reading this book you decide you want to learn more about some of the specific topics presented, I would recommend *Drive*, by Daniel Pink; *Conscious Capitalism*, by Whole Foods Market Co-CEO John Mackey and Raj

Sisodia; *Delivering Happiness*, by Zappos CEO Tony Hsieh; *Good Boss, Bad Boss*, by Stanford University's Robert Sutton; *Rediscovering Values*, by Jim Wallis; and *Louder Than Words*, by Bob Kelleher.

There is an overwhelming amount of resources and literature on the topic of employee engagement. However, if you are looking for an evidence-based engagement strategy that benefits both your corporation and community at the same time, keep reading.

Choosing Citizen-centered Leadership

We've all felt a loss of control over our lives, but haven't been quite sure how to get it back. We've all felt disappointment in our elected officials, but haven't stepped forward to do it ourselves. And lastly, we've all felt the emptiness corporate America offers, because after all, most of us spend the majority of our waking hours at work. We've all felt a loss of citizenship.

My intent is to inspire both our current and next generation of leaders to lead in a remarkable way that breaks through today's status quo that is driving no-longer-acceptable levels of engagement at work and community; as well as invigorate employees of all ranks to adopt a new set of expectations for their leaders.

Why can't America revisit the ties that once held corporation and community closely together? It absolutely can. When our leaders choose citizen-centered leadership.

"Never doubt that a small group of thoughtful

committed citizens can change the world;

indeed, it's the only thing that ever has."

MARGARET MEAD

TIES THAT BIND

Being on or near the water has always been my escape from a hectic schedule and endless deadlines at work. Research not only shows water's calming effects, but also health benefits and creative thinking. This time spent on the water has introduced me to two things: The fun and contagious lyrics of Jimmy Buffett, and my husband's Bob Bitchin book collection.

Civilization Rediscovered

In *Letters from the Lost Soul*, author Bob Bitchin writes about his travels aboard his sailboat named the Lost Soul. During one of his many adventures, he rediscovers civilization on the uncivilized Polynesian island of Suvarov. Upon the Lost Soul's arrival, the island's resident caretaker, Ioane, immediately extends to the crew, "When you visit our island you are family." Bitchin goes on to say about this particular discovery:

> For every night we stayed in Suvarov, they had a barbecue for us and any other boaters that came in. No charge, just lots of coconut crabs, lobsters, fish, and breadfruit. During the day they would invite us to dive with them, or go fishing, or to visit the outlying

motus. We would fish, or dive, and catch what we'd eat that night for supper. Of course we would bring in canned fruits or vegetables, but they didn't need them. They made some of the greatest tasting food from the plants found right on the island.

Bitchin notes in his book that he especially enjoyed the company of Ioane, and wondered how two men of completely different interests and backgrounds – Bitchin, a sailor and ex-biker, and Ioane, an old islander who had never seen television – could have such common understanding, feeling like kindred spirits. Bitchin attributes the camaraderie by stating, "Different backgrounds, but equal values." He asks Ioane how he could repay him in some way for his hospitality, and Ioane responded by saying the appreciation he could see in the eyes of Bitchin's crew was more than payment. Bitchin journaled this experience in a compelling way by stating:

It seems that in the true Polynesian culture, the thing that makes a person get a good feeling inside, "warm fuzzies," is to do something for others. The fact that he can help another person makes his day. Those in the civilized world seem to get the same feeling from knowing they have bested someone, or taken advantage. The simplicity of the life on these "uncivilized" islands makes what we'd lived with at home seem gross, crass, and almost criminal. As we lived in that society, all that we'd left back home seemed unreal, like a bad dream, a nightmare. Now that we have returned to civilization, what we lived out there seems to be a dream. But a good one. One we yearn to return to. And that is the difference. If there was just one day, one hour, that had more effect on me than any other in my life, it would be one day I spent on Suvarov Island.

The "Good Dream"

Bitchin's accounting of Suvarov begs the question, *Have we lost sight of the ties that bind us as Americans?* President Barack Obama ended his 2013 State of the Union address with words designed to close the political party divide. However, I think the words he chose do more than that. Whether you are a democrat, republican, or independent; blue collar or white collar; Protestant, Catholic or Buddhist, his words encapsulated our common ideals – perhaps the *good dream* Bitchin yearns to return to. Here is what President Obama said:

We may do different jobs, and wear different uniforms, and hold different views than the person beside us. But as Americans, we all share the same proud title: We are citizens. It's a word that doesn't just describe our nationality or legal status. It describes the way we're made. It describes what we believe. It captures the enduring idea that this country

only works when we accept certain obligations to one another and to future genera-
tions; that our rights are wrapped up in the
rights of others; and that well into our third
century as a nation, it remains the task of us
all, as citizens of these United States, to be
the authors of the next great chapter in our
American story.

These important ties that bind us together can best be
summarized as *citizenship*. This book is about our obligations
as leaders and achieving our common ideals as citizens. Think
of it this way. Every leader has both the choice and opportunity to turn his or her organization into Suvarov Island. Just like
a pristine beach waiting to be rediscovered, America's social
capital can once again be revived when leaders are willing to
return to the core principles that once tied people, businesses
and community together.

It's time to take off your shoes, feel the sand between your
toes and take your first step.

CORPORATE & COMMUNITY DISENGAGEMENT

The current state of our workplace is disheartening. According to Gallup Group, 70 percent of Americans who go to work every day are not engaged in their job. And when you boil it down, some studies have shown that only 6 percent are highly engaged. Based on research conducted by

THE COST OF ACTIVELY DISENGAGED WORKERS TO THE U.S. ECONOMY IS ESTIMATED AT $450 TO $550 BILLION ANNUALLY.

Towers Watson, engagement levels in 2010 represented the largest decline in 15 years. Why does it matter? The cost of actively disengaged workers to the U.S. economy is estimated at $450 to $550 billion annually.

Dollars and Sense

A Harvard University Kennedy School of Government report from the Saguaro Seminar on Civic Engagement in America, *Better Together*, is clear in pointing out the financial benefits of strong social capital, indicating research has begun to show how powerfully social capital, or its absence, affects the well being of individuals, organizations and nations. The definition of social capital is *connections within and between social networks.* Economic studies demonstrate that social capital makes workers more productive, firms more competitive and nations more prosperous.

Key drivers of employee engagement link to the existence of social capital in corporations, including actions of senior leadership, actions of supervisors, belief in vision and values, and fostering of a people culture. Gallup's extensive research shows engagement is strongly connected to business outcomes essential to an organization's financial success, including productivity, quality of products and customer satisfaction. If companies can successfully engage their employees, the benefits are significant:

- Companies with highly engaged employees experience 19.2 percent higher operating income, 17 percent higher operating margin, and 27.8 percent improvement in earnings per share. However, within companies with disengaged employees, employees are absent 3.5 more days per year, experience a decreased operating income of 32.7 percent and a 3.8 percent decline in net income, as well as an 11.2 percent decline in earnings per share.

- Aon Hewitt's research also shows a strong correlation between employee engagement and financial performance. Organizations with high levels of engagement continue to outperform the total stock market index and posted total shareholder returns 22 percent higher than average in 2010. Companies with low engagement had a total shareholder return 28 percent lower than average.

- Employees who are most committed to their organizations put forth 57 percent more effort and were 87 percent less likely to leave their company than employees who considered themselves disengaged.

- And last, companies ranked in the "100 Best Companies to Work For" experience half the voluntary turnover rate of companies that are not on the list.

This seems like something worth investing in, yes? However, as a country, we must not be making the right investment or we aren't making any investment at all.

Corporations historically have used employee surveys to understand levels of engagement. Today, an increasing number are leveraging the surveys to better understand *what* drives engagement. These drivers guide new corporate policies, or refinement to existing policies, that can improve both morale *and* the bottom line. Even though employee engagement surveys have become more widely used and sophisticated in their application, research reveals while

ONLY ONE IN FOUR LEADERS HAVE AN ENGAGEMENT PLAN OR STRATEGY IN PLACE.

90 percent of leaders recognize employee engagement is still the most crucial factor for organizational success; *only one in four leaders have an engagement plan or strategy in place.*

Community Disengagement

What shouldn't be shocking is that low engagement in our workplaces can also be found in our communities. Put another way, the same people who wake up to the rushed and hectic daily routine that corporate America offers, go home at night and aren't engaged in community-building activities. Or at least they aren't as engaged as they could be…or used to be.

Robert Putnam's research in *Bowling Alone* reveals America's significant decline in citizen engagement over the last several decades. According to Putnam, the core of our most civic generation was born between 1925-1930, attended grade school during the Great Depression, spent World War II in high school (or on the battlefield), first voted in 1948 or 1952, set up housekeeping in the 1950s, and saw their first television when they were in their late twenties. According to Putnam, "Since national polling began, this cohort has been exceptionally civic – voting more, joining more, reading more, trusting more, giving more."

> CITIZEN ENGAGEMENT HAS SIGNIFICANTLY DECLINED OVER THE LAST SEVERAL DECADES.

How our society interacts and functions has changed in so many ways – ways that used to promote and build social capital. Putnam attributes the erosion of these ties to: (1) The pressures of time and money, specifically as the result of two-career families; (2) Suburbanization, commuting and sprawl; (3) The effect electronic entertainment (most notably television) has had on privatizing our leisure time, rather than walking over to the neighbors or participating in clubs; and (4) Most importantly, generational change.

According to Putnam, all of these factors combined have contributed to less commune and socialization with neighbors, less community involvement, fewer family dinners, lower church and club meeting attendance, fewer people reading the newspaper, reduced participation in politics, less frequent organized leisure activities, and so on.

More specifically, Putnam's research indicates:

> Family dinners and family vacations or even just sitting and talking with your family are down by one third in the last 25 years.

> The number of socially isolated Americans has more than doubled over the 2 decades from 1984-2004 from 10 percent to 25 percent of all Americans.

> Having friends over to the house is down by 45 percent over the last 25 years.

> Participation in clubs and civic organizations has been cut by more than half over the last 25 years.

Involvement in community life, such as public meetings is down by 35 percent over the
last 25 years.

Church attendance is down by roughly one
third since the 1960s.

Philanthropy as fraction of income is down
by nearly one third since the 1960s.

Just like corporations, when communities have high
social capital, they thrive. People in communities work
better together, are safer, healthier, happier and overall rely
less on the need for government interventions and services.
Strong social capital creates higher functioning systems in
education, economies and governments.

A High-tech, Low-touch World

We live in a highly competitive, technology-driven society. There is a lot to be gained by being the most innovative and cutting edge; but conversely, a lot to be lost when it
comes to workplace culture and our communities. Continued
advances in technology have opened many doors to easily
connect with others across the globe; however, these same
advances can also contribute to solitude.

People working remotely results in less face-to-face communication that's required in building trust, interpersonal understanding and relationships in the workplace. A smile, body
language, and even voice tone is lost through email and text

message communication, even though those mediums are heavily relied upon in today's corporate world. It is often times used as a primary way to manage employees *(management by email)* as well as facilitate important decision making. Even before the internet and television, Putnam attributes early disintegration of social capital to the emergence of the telephone.

Community-building author, Peter Block, describes our society's high-tech, low-touch dilemma this way:

> Ironically, we talk today of how small our world has become, with the shrinking effect of globalization, instant sharing of information, quick technology, workplaces that operate around the globe. Yet these do not necessarily create a sense of belonging. They provide connection, diverse information, an infinite range of opinion. But all this does not create the connection from which we can become grounded and experience the sense of safety that arises from a place where we are emotionally, spiritually, and psychologically a member.

Not Enough Time

Today's dilemma of reduced social capital can also be described as *not enough time.* By one estimate, the average American worker clocks up to 40 percent more hours during his life time than the average person in Germany, France or Italy. In 2009, married middle-income parents worked the equivalent of an additional day a week (8.6

hours) – almost 12 additional weeks - as compared to 1979.

TODAY'S DILEMMA OF REDUCED SOCIAL CAPITAL CAN ALSO BE DESCRIBED AS NOT ENOUGH TIME.

We live in a society where it's easier to give money than time, or become a mailing list member of the Sierra Club rather than having to go to club meetings. It's perhaps easier to pay higher property taxes so that the Joneses have someone to come check on them once a week when they get older, so we don't have to. However, when the economy is in a downturn, we may no longer be in a position to give money. We may not have a healthy tax base to lean on. So then what are we left with? *Where are the ties that bind us?*

Urban sprawl has significantly elongated the amount of time it takes for us to get to and from work, thus reducing our time with family, neighbors and community. Dual-working homes exacerbate this issue of drive time, in that sometimes both spouses are unable to find work that aligns with their career path in the same community. A large portion of workers may also be caring for not only their children, but also their aging parents. Again, *not enough time.*

A New Generation

Combined with pressures surrounding time, as Putnam suggests, we can't overlook how generational change has contributed to our social capital decline. The baby boomers, our largest generation in American history, were raised by parents who survived the Great Depression and World War II. As a result, they taught their children to give generously both in time and money. But today, Gen X (born in the early 60s through the early 80s) and Gen Y (born in the early 80s through early 2000s) are looking for different things when it comes to memberships and associations. Their motivation to join wasn't engrained in them during their most formative years as it was with their parents. And because of their limited time, they are choosier about what they will invest themselves in. They need to be able to see measurable outcomes. They need to know that what they are investing in is truly making an impact. Many in the X and Y generation are turned off by organizations created and led by boomers with traditional due structures, offering little in the way of meaningful membership benefits.

A large number of non-profit organizations and associations with a boomer culture still exist today, but have stumbled in successfully establishing relevance with our new generation's requirement of high value and desire to see results before they are willing to engage.

Center of Our Universe

Because the average American spends most of their waking hours on the job, employment is central to a person's community. It is the center of our meaning and support structure. When we introduce ourselves to someone new, it's most often one of the first things we say about ourselves to describe who we are. Ironically though as the *Better Together* report states, the workplace plays a dual social capital role – nurturing it in some ways, and draining it in others.

Employment determines where we live, what kind of home we live in, the prospect of how long we will live in a community, how many hours we are at work, and essentially what daily schedule we keep. So whether you're a CEO of a large corporation or the owner of a local grocery store, you play a significant role in influencing the lives of others and essentially shaping your community. Stanford University's Bob Sutton wrote a book about what constitutes a good boss versus bad boss and perhaps

THE WORKPLACE PLAYS A DUAL SOCIAL CAPITAL ROLE – NURTURING IT IN SOME WAYS, AND DRAINING IT IN OTHERS.

summed it up best by stating, "Bosses shape how people spend their days and whether they experience joy or despair, perform well or badly, or are healthy or sick."

When we think about employment as the center of our universe, it's important to note that employees do not spend the majority of their career with one employer as in the past. This loss of loyalty isn't necessarily a byproduct of increased mobility and more employment options. There is a reason why workers have become less loyal to employers over recent decades – employers have also become less loyal to them. Stealing employees from competitors or rapid downsizing many times is used to grow or maintain profit margins rather than investing in the existing corporate family.

We work in an environment where anyone and everyone are considered replaceable. But are we really? Consider the other assets we bring to the workplace other than our skill and education. First, we bring the wealth of tacit knowledge that we've gained from that organization as the result of working there. Whether its knowing department processes, organizational trade secrets or having close and trusting relationships with coworkers, other departments and business partners, there's a significant knowledge base lost when a person leaves an organization.

When you look at both the direct costs (costs associated with recruitment, hiring, training, temporary coverage, etc.) and indirect costs (loss of productivity, increased errors, lost clients, etc.) of replacing an employee, the cost is estimated to be one-fifth of an employee's salary. Executive positions are estimated to cost significantly more, estimated at over 200 percent of an executive's annual salary. Let's say we're dealing with

THE BENEFITS OF INVESTING IN SOCIAL CAPITAL ARE NOT UNDERSTOOD OR APPRECIATED BY TODAY'S LEADER.

an organization of 20,000 employees. If the average employee's pay with benefits is $70,000, at a 15 percent turnover rate the annual cost to the organization would be $42 million.

Let's not forget we also bring our existing ties and contributions to community, potentially including the ties of a spouse and/or children. When you take all of these important variables into consideration – relationships, tacit knowledge, replacement costs, community ties, and family ties – in reality we are extremely difficult to replace in both corporation and community. So why is it we feel so dispensable?

Here's why. When it comes to attracting, engaging, and retaining talent - the second-most important business challenge facing CEOs today - *the level of priority compared to other business investments is ranked at 44.* The benefits of investing in social capital are not understood or appreciated by today's leader.

STATE OF THE UNION

On both fronts, community and corporation, the data reveals Americans are not currently empowered to exercise their full potential. Public theologian Reverend Jim Wallis critiques our current culture by stating, "It's time to stop keeping up with the Joneses and start making sure the Joneses are okay." At a time when our nation is recovering from the deepest recession in decades, not only are the vast majority of Americans disengaged, but we also have never been more economically divided.

> **NOT ONLY ARE THE VAST MAJORITY OF AMERICANS DISENGAGED, BUT WE ALSO HAVE NEVER BEEN MORE ECONOMICALLY DIVIDED.**

A Divided Society

America's largest corporation, Walmart, is an example for us to consider. At $17.5 million annually, former CEO Lee Scott Jr. made 900 times more than the average Walmart employee. Said another way, Mr. Scott made in two weeks what his average employee would make in a lifetime. Scott's salary pales in comparison to the Walton's family wealth, estimated at $90 billion (Sam Walton was the founder of Walmart).

In Wallis' book, *Rediscovering Values: On main street, wall street, and your street,* Wallis compares wage growth since the post-World War II boom when we were most engaged as citizens, and only the top 1 percent have done better. "The richer you are, the better it gets. The top one-tenth of one percent saw their incomes increase five times over, and the top one-hundredth of one percent is seven times richer than they were in 1973," says Wallis. Even after adjusting for inflation, Wallis indicates:

> ...the value of the per-hour output of the average worker has risen almost 50 percent since 1973. If these gains in productivity had been evenly shared across the workforce, the typical worker's income would be about 35 percent higher now than it was in the early 1970s. To put it differently, if the typical household had shared evenly in the productivity gains, they would have earned about $20,000 more in 2006 than they actually did.

A 2012 Economic Policy Institute study shows the top 1 percent of households holding a larger share of overall wealth than the bottom 90 percent. This concentration of wealth might not only translate to economic inequality, but instead economists are now saying it also creates sluggish growth and economic instability for our nation. In fact, recent research indicates four out of five U.S. adults struggle with joblessness, near-poverty or reliance on

FOUR OUT OF FIVE U.S. ADULTS STRUGGLE WITH JOBLESSNESS, NEAR-POVERTY OR RELIANCE ON WELFARE FOR AT LEAST PARTS OF THEIR LIVES.

welfare for at least parts of their lives– a clear sign of deteriorating economic security.

The Compensation Conversation

A key driver of wage inequality is the growth of chief executive compensation. From 1978–2011, CEO compensation grew more than 725 percent, substantially more than the stock market and remarkably more than worker compensation at a meager 5.7 percent. The CEO-to-worker compensation ratio in 2011 was 209.4-to-1, compared to 18.3-to-1 in 1965. This illustrates that CEOs have fared far better than the typical worker, the stock market, or the U.S. economy over the last several decades. Across the Standard and Poor's 500 Index of companies, you'll find over 200 companies that come in over the 200-to-1 ratio, topping as high as 1,795-to-1 with stock options.

Economist Robert Reich served in three national administrations, most recently as secretary of labor under President Clinton. According to Reich, Americans have accepted this lack of wage growth by mitigating its effects. The American middle class developed three coping mechanisms as a way to take home the same share of total income and maintain the same ability to spend: 1) Women moved into paid work; 2) We work longer hours; and 3) We draw down savings and borrow to the hilt. Reich says not until these coping mechanisms finally became exhausted in the Great Recession did this underlying reality of inequality become evident. It seems we may not be engaging because we are too busy coping.

Operational Performance

Literature has shown when CEOs are given significantly higher pay and power than their direct reports, these gaps are linked to lower company performance. If workers shared more in the fruits of their labor would they be more engaged?

> **IF WORKERS SHARED MORE IN THE FRUITS OF THEIR LABOR WOULD THEY BE MORE ENGAGED?**

Popular management author Peter Drucker focused his work on relationships among people. He insisted in over 70 years of authorship that a CEO-to-worker compensation ratio of 25-to-1, or even 20-to-1, was the appropriate balance to ensure sound business as well as good morale. He felt excessively high ratios undermined teamwork and promoted a winner-takes-all culture.

Natural and organic foods grocer, Whole Foods Market, follows Drucker's framework. Across the entire organization (340 stores in North America and the United Kingdom), Whole Foods Market follows a policy that caps total cash compensation for any team member at 19 times the average pay of all team members. Co-CEO John Mackey compares this with publicly traded companies of similar size, where this ratio can be as high as 400-500 times. Additionally, all seven members of the executive leadership team are paid the same, creating solidarity and a high degree of trust within that group. Mackey admits you can make the case that some executives are more valuable than others, but that differences in compensation can "stoke envy and erode trust." Above that, he says the organization's leaders have a strong sense of calling, which supersedes the need to have their self-worth validated by money.

From time to time Whole Foods Market has had to resist the efforts of certain leaders in the company who felt they deserved better benefits than others because they were in a higher position. Eventually, those leaders left the company to chase more money, and in each case, Mackey says the organization was happy to see them go. "We were able to replace them with more capable leaders who aligned better with our culture. For Whole Foods Market, the issue is non-negotiable," says Mackey. He feels the organization's overall compensation approach attracts people with a higher degree of emotional intelligence. To maintain the spirit of the 19-to-1 ratio, Mackey donates income from his personal stock options to Whole Food's two non-profit foundations.

Compensation Considerations

Conversations surrounding compensation are not about republican or democratic ideology, or capitalism versus socialism. The purpose of discussing these gaps is to help us better understand connections between compensation, engagement, organizational performance and our economy. As a free-enterprise capitalist nation, as citizens we have the ability to augment our economic environment in a way that benefits both people *and* business.

According to Wharton School finance expert and Fortune 500 business consultant R. Paul Herman, the CEO-to-employee compensation ratio is an important investment consideration. Herman created the HIP (Human Impact + Profit) investment methodology as way of steering American investors away from practices and cultures that remain focused on short-term returns, toward profitable companies that contribute toward a sustainable America. He offers investment metrics to use in evaluating which companies are top performers, and a key metric is the CEO's compensation relative to average staff pay. For an overall portfolio, he calculates that a lower ratio correlates to higher levels of financial performance.

Psychological studies surrounding engagement touch upon this same topic, showing in today's economy high CEO compensation does not correlate with high company performance, but instead high ego. According to industrial psychology experts David Bowles and Cary Cooper, ego and engagement are polar opposites: engagement is about *we* and ego is about *me*. Their work confirms that business performance deteriorates when pay differentials become excessive. In a study of over 100 diverse businesses, they found the greater the wage gap between managers and workers, the lower their product's quality. Also, businesses with the greatest inequality were fraught with high employee turnover rates.

Organizations with higher manager-to-worker pay ratios aren't able to sustain a workplace built upon the foundation of shared goals. They aren't able to create a *we're-all-in-this-together* culture. It takes all hands within an organization to achieve its goals. If there is a perception that CEO pay is too high, a connotation exists that the CEO is predominantly responsible for organizational success.

As you are reading this, you may be reflecting upon other literature that you've read indicating employee pay isn't always a key factor when employees decide to stay or leave an organization. You're right. However, the point made here is surrounding trust and equity. Much like a wealthy political candidate running for office, how does it impact how voters relate to him or her? A workforce must be able to relate to its leader in order

ORGANIZATIONS WITH HIGHER MANAGER-TO-WORKER PAY RATIOS AREN'T ABLE TO SUSTAIN A WORKPLACE BUILT UPON THE FOUNDATION OF SHARED GOALS.

for the leader to obtain respect, but more importantly, trust.

When thousands of exit surveys were analyzed from a Saratoga study, a fundamental un-met human need was identified as a root cause of when employees begin to think about leaving an organization. It was the need for trust, which was defined as expecting the company and management to deliver on its promises to be honest and open in all communications, to invest in you, to treat you fairly, and to compensate you fairly and on time.

YOUR LEADERSHIP PURSUIT

Every once in a while a story will hit the media because of leadership by an out-of-the-ordinary CEO, such as the City National Bank of Florida in 2008. Bank President Leonard Abess cashed out of his company, took a $60 million bonus, and gave it out to all 399 people who worked for him, *plus another 72 who used to work for him.* He didn't tell anyone, but when the local newspaper found out, he simply said, "I knew some of these people since I was 7 years old. I didn't feel right getting the money myself."

The Pursuit of Bob and Charlee Moore

Bob's Red Mill, based out of Milwaukie, Oregon, offers whole grain foods with a diverse line of all natural, organic and gluten-free flours, cereals, meals and mixes for breads, cakes, soups and pancakes. In 2010, owner Bob Moore celebrated his 81st birthday with an announcement he had been waiting years to make. He told his employees that Bob's Red Mill was now an employee-owned company and 200-plus employees were presented with a new employee stock ownership plan. "It's been my dream all along to turn this company over to the employees, and to make that dream a reality on my birthday is just the icing on the cake," said Moore, who founded the company with his wife Charlee in 1978. Management announced the new employee stock ownership plan at an all-company meeting at their headquarters in Oregon.

"To me, this is the ultimate way to reward employees for their contributions to our ongoing success and growth. We have many loyal and long-time employees who I expect will be joined by many new faces over the years to run the company," said Bob's Red Mill Operations Vice President Dennis Vaughn. The Moore's could have sold the company many times for a lot more money, but to them the company was about more than money.

A Management Revolution

City National Bank of Florida and Bob's Red Mill share a common theme - a sense of community and belonging. The Management Lab, a Silicon Valley non-profit research organization that focuses on management innovation, recently pulled together 35 management scholars and practitioners who met for two days to debate the future of management. They were tasked with providing an answer to what great challenges must we tackle to reinvent management and make it more relevant to a volatile world. While they all held their own specific frustrations with today's management culture, they agreed on one thing: In order for organizations to successfully tackle the future, *it would require a management revolution as momentous as the one that spawned modern industry.* Collectively they came up with 25 moonshots for management...second on the list was that *we need to embed community and citizenship into management systems.*

As a leader, you have a tremendous opportunity to be a part of this revolution. Through the culture you choose for your organization, you can influence social capital to benefit your organization, community, and ultimately our country. As our nation attempted to recover lost economic ground during the Great Recession, Jim Wallis (quoted in Chapter 2) said our nation was at a critical juncture.

> **THROUGH THE CULTURE YOU CHOOSE FOR YOUR ORGANIZATION, YOU CAN INFLUENCE SOCIAL CAPITAL TO BENEFIT YOUR ORGANIZATION, COMMUNITY, AND ULTIMATELY OUR COUNTRY.**

"We need to decide whether the purpose of business and the vocation of our business leaders is restricted to turning a profit or if it can become something more," he said. As economists made predictions of when and how quickly the economy would recover, Wallis said the worst thing we could wish for is for things to go back to the way they were. I agree. It's clear we need to change the way we think about people, organizations and communities. This means we need to change the way we think about leadership.

Citizen-centered Leadership

Through citizen-centered leadership you accept – and embrace – the significance of tens, hundreds, maybe thousands of loyal workers counting on you. These loyal workers - or citizens - make up the broader community where you live. When executives recognize and appreciate this, their leadership pursuit changes. In *Conscious Capitalism*, authors Raj Sisodia and Whole Foods Market Co-CEO John Mackey summarize the impact leaders have on all of our lives:

> Leadership matters a great deal, and the reason it matters is broader than organizational performance. The quality of our leaders affects the quality of our lives. Every good leader contributes in ways, big and small, toward making the world a better place – one day, one life, and one company at a time.

There are thousands of books and publications on how to become an effective leader, which are followed up by leadership programs in all shapes and sizes. What are my strengths? How do I effectively build and lead teams? How can I learn more about myself as a leader? But for the most part, today's trend in leadership materials skirt around the core issue of the deterioration of social capital, how to rebuild it, and corporate leadership's opportunity and responsibility to lead in this area.

How many books have you read about leadership that created intrigue, but had little impact or sustaining change in how you choose to lead? How many offered you a platform to influence the lives of others in a meaningful way? Citizen-centered leadership is different. It's simple, yet significant. It is about getting America back to the basics and restoring what's most important to Americans – having work with purpose, having the time to do things in life that we want to, and raising our families the way we think they should be raised. It's about priorities, values and reviving community within a new construct and generation that exists today. Citizen-centered leadership builds upon Ioane's joy of giving to others, versus beating out others. We demonstrate this inherent human preference as toddlers. Happiness is felt most when you're helping others versus taking something for yourself.

As a cornerstone to your leadership pursuit, much like the constitution of a nation you need ideological clarity. You must answer the questions of, *Why are we here? What is it we want to accomplish collectively?* And, just as importantly, *How will we get there together?* This clarity reveals the *kind* of people who are best suited to work for your corporate cause. When this alignment between corporate cause and hiring is right, work becomes more than a job, and in-

ONLY WHEN THE ROLE OF SOCIAL CAPITAL IS UNDERSTOOD, IT BECOMES THE DRIVING VARIABLE IN YOUR LEADERSHIP PURSUIT.

stead a calling. Be deliberate in defining the culture you want, hire for that culture; but then our work as leaders does not end. We must nurture and feed that culture much in the same way thriving communities nurture and feed themselves.

If you are reading this book and wondering if it holds insight that can help you, ask yourself these three questions. *Do I feel my organization is capable of producing improved operational results? Have I become increasingly concerned that customers aren't happy? Do my employees like working for me or like their work?*

While you may have the expertise and training needed to make sound business decisions in your respective field, you may be lacking the core leadership competencies that build and sustain high social capital. Here's the secret though, it isn't your fault. Because until now, you have been rewarded through accolades and promotions to keep doing what you are doing. Why would you do anything different?

What you need to know is that this is where your advantage lies as an organization. Leaders who pride themselves on high intellectual know-how often struggle with accepting or admitting this. Many executives and managers rely on more tangible and traditional areas in the pursuit of competitive advantage, such as strategic planning, technology investments, marketing tactics or the latest in process improvement techniques. Sometimes it's tinkering with the org chart, changing out staff or administering more controls. Only

IF WE'VE SUCCESSFULLY CHANGED THE WAY WE THINK ABOUT PEOPLE, ORGANIZATIONS AND COMMUNITIES, THEN OUR NEXT STEP IS REDEFINING OUR WORK AS LEADERS.

when the role of social capital is understood, it becomes the driving variable in your leadership pursuit.

If you are feeling bold and feel open to trying something different - because you want improved financial performance, you want customers who can't wait to tell their family and friends about your product or service, you want your workforce to like working for you, you want to be a part of an economic stimulus package that doesn't contribute to national debt - this book introduces a new set of core competencies that we should expect from all of our leaders. These competencies make up the ingredients for better organizations *and* communities. Because as you will discover, organizations and communities are one in the same.

Redefining the Work of Leadership

If we've successfully changed the way we think about people, organizations and communities, then our next step is redefining our work as leaders. The Management Lab's 35 management scholars also suggested that in the future management model leaders will be seen much differently than they are today. Leaders will no longer be seen as grand visionaries, all-wise decision makers, and ironfisted disciplinarians; but instead, they will need to become *social architects, constitution writers, and entrepreneurs of meaning.*

Chapters 4, 5 and 6 present a clear and compelling framework for the citizen-centered leader. One who sees themselves as perhaps one of the future social architects, constitution writers and entrepreneurs of meaning. One who knows how to build social capital resulting in highly engaged employees and citizens. One who is willing to do the hard work after the mission statement is written.

You will be introduced to organizations - large and small, new and old - with brands built upon a solid foundation of community. The following eight steps provide you with your roadmap to become a part of the management revolution by turning workplaces into communities and employees into citizens. Let's begin a conversation about how to ensure mission statements hold meaning by rebuilding workplace cultures and our communities one leader at a time.

VALUES &
IDEOLOGICAL CLARITY

Step 1 – Draft your company constitution.

Many corporations operate in a dog-eat-dog atmosphere of competing executives working to achieve individual wins, primarily for promotional purposes, but sometimes for job security when the work environment lacks stability. Disrespectful behavior and the goal of beating out others is a byproduct of this work environment, in addition to lack of teamwork. This kind of environment may create short-term wins, but in actuality is disruptive to the organization and long-term gains. If we want a civil society, expect civility in government and from elected officials, then why would we allow anything different in our workplace?

Beyond the Mission Statement

I have heard many Americans discuss at length how they do not feel they can trust anyone at work. In other words, they do not feel there are others in their organization looking out for their best interests – many times including their immediate supervisor. This results in a work environment of solitude, loneliness and isolation.

Corporate executives need to hold their workforce to a standard that promotes the facilitation of positive and respectful relationships. Without it, social capital won't perpetuate and build, instead it quickly sputters out. To guide this effort, we certainly all have mission statements, but what about value statements? Aside from what the organizational goal is, what is the accepted and collectively agreed-upon philosophy of getting there? What is your constitution? Are these constitutional values modeled by the CEO and executive cabinet? Middle management? How an organization or department gets there is just as important as getting there.

> **IF WE WANT A CIVIL SOCIETY, EXPECT CIVILITY IN GOVERNMENT AND FROM ELECTED OFFICIALS, THEN WHY WOULD WE ALLOW ANYTHING DIFFERENT IN OUR WORKPLACE?**

In Bob Sutton's book about good and bad bosses, he includes a testimonial from one of his own experiences. It reinforces the point that the leader of an organization matters more than the other bosses and must be the first to follow the constitution:

> The top dog sets the tone for how his or her direct reports behave - which reverberates through the system. I worked with a large company where the CEO did almost all the talking in meetings, interrupted anyone who tried to get in a word edgewise, and aggressively silenced any underling who voiced a dissenting view. The executive vice presidents on his senior team complained bitterly

(behind his back, of course) about the antics of their bossy boss. But I noticed that as soon as the CEO left the room, the most powerful EVP started acting exactly like his boss. Then, when that EVP departed, the next highest-ranking boss remaining in the room began mimicking the CEOs overbearing style. It was fascinating to watch this behavior travel down the local pecking order.

Consider putting the company constitution up on the wall in the cafeteria, maybe on the company letterhead, or company screensaver. The point is, everyone needs to know what it is. There's only one caveat – you have to follow it. The constitution then becomes the bedrock for every human process used by the organization – internal and external communication, hiring and firing, customer interactions, compensation structure, performance evaluations, etc.

> **THE CONSTITUTION THEN BECOMES THE BEDROCK FOR EVERY HUMAN PROCESS USED BY THE ORGANIZATION.**

The Horny Toad Constitution

California-based Horny Toad clothing's mantra is *Look Good. Feel Good. Do Good*, where leadership states:

> The choices we make are as important as the clothes we create. We try each day to lighten our environmental footprint, be good partners in all of our relationships, pay attention

and stay active in our communities and support organizations that improve our world - the source of our daily adventures.

Horny Toad's constitution includes:

INNOVATION in our products, brand, culture, partnerships and way we approach business.

RESPECT for the ideas, perspectives and needs of customers, employees, our community, supply partners and the industry as a whole.

LEADERSHIP by example with self-awareness, confidence and humility.

RESPONSIBILITY to do the right thing.

CURIOSITY with a dedication to listen, understand, learn and improve.

COMMITMENT to the vision, getting to the best answer, taking action and achieving results.

BALANCE in all aspects of our lives to maintain a healthy, happy and high performing state of mind.

One example of how the company's constitution comes to life is in how it chooses to deliver its products. With my first Horny Toad purchase, I noticed on the tag it indicated all *Toads* were packed and shipped by an organization that employs people with disabilities, whose profits go toward services for the disabled. The tag states, "When Horny Toad met Search, Inc. in 1997, a Chicago-based social service agency, they fell in love with the common goal of doing the right thing." Horny Toad makes great products, but knowing this gave me even more reason to become brand loyal. The right customers will seek out businesses that are serious about their constitution.

Your Constitution and Hiring

When Zappos CEO Tony Hsieh moved his company headquarters to Las Vegas in 2003, the company was hiring a lot of people because of rapid growth. Hsieh could no longer be involved in all hiring decisions. Because there were so many new hires already on board, when Hsieh would say, *We need a good culture fit,* others weren't necessarily up to speed on what that really meant – in practical terms. So that's exactly what he did. Hsieh thought about all of the employees that he said he wanted to clone, because they represented the Zappos culture well, and determined what values they personified most.

He started a list, which initially was made up of 37 values. After receiving feedback from employees, they came up with their final list of 10 core values, which they still adhere to today:

1. Deliver WOW Through Service
2. Embrace and Drive Change
3. Create Fun and a Little Weirdness
4. Be Adventurous, Creative, and Open-Minded
5. Pursue Growth and Learning
6. Build Open and Honest Relationships with Communication
7. Build a Positive Team and Family Spirit
8. Do More with Less
9. Be Passionate and Determined
10. Be Humble

Hsieh says the last value – *Be Humble* – is a value that ends up affecting hiring decisions the most. "There are a lot of experienced, smart, and talented people we interview that we know can make an immediate impact on our top or bottom line. But a lot of them are also really egotistical, so we end up not hiring them," says Hsieh.

Hsieh feels most corporations would hire this *type* because of the immediate value they would add, but Hsieh goes on to say, "Our philosophy at Zappos is that we're willing to make short-term sacrifices (including lost revenue or profits) if we believe that the long-term benefits are worth it. Protecting the company culture and sticking to core values is a long-term benefit." Hseih uses the core values to reflect all actions of the company, including how employees interact with one another, how the company interacts with customers, and interactions with vendors and business partners. I experienced Value #1 - *Wow* - when I ordered a pair of shoes at 11 p.m. one night and found them on my doorstep when I returned from work the very next day, without having paid anything for shipping.

Just as important as telling applicants what you are, you need to be able to articulate what you aren't. If part of your constitution is aspirational – a work in progress – then you need to be transparent with applicants regarding where the organization stands. Remember, the goal is to attract employees who are the best fit. If honesty isn't present during the interview process, then you've just hired someone whose first reaction to the organization is disappointment, resentment and lack of trust.

Walking the Talk

There's nothing worse than an organization that has taken all of the measures just described and then doesn't walk the talk - reinforcing and rewarding the right behaviors, and facilitating an environment of accountability. Reinforcement can be seen at its best during hiring and firing. It's just as important to hire employees with the right values as it is to get rid of the ones without them.

In a General Electric annual letter to shareholders, during a key transition time for the company, leadership said they wanted to "...reflect on what GE is today: why it works, the values and beliefs it is built upon and how they will serve to take us to the even better days that we know lie ahead for our company." The letter further explained how the organization would stay aligned to its constitution through the difficult decision of removing those who do not belong:

It's about the four "E's" we've been using for years as a screen to pick our leaders. "Energy:"

To cope with the frenetic pace of change. "Energize:" The ability to excite, to galvanize the organization and inspire it to action. "Edge:" The self-confidence to make the tough calls, with "yeses" and "noes" - and very few "maybes." And "Execute:" The ancient GE tradition of always delivering, never disappointing.

And it's about the four "types" that represent the way we evaluate and deal with our existing leaders. Type I: Shares our values; makes the numbers - sky's the limit! Type II: Doesn't share the values; doesn't make the numbers - gone. Type III: Shares the values; misses the numbers - typically, another chance, or two.

None of these three are tough calls, but Type IV is the toughest call of all: The manager who doesn't share the values, but delivers the numbers; the "go-to" manager, the hammer, who delivers the bacon but does it on the backs of people, often "kissing up and kicking down" during the process. This type is the toughest to part with because organizations always want to deliver - it's in the blood - and to let someone go who gets the job done is yet another unnatural act. But we have to remove these Type IV's because they have the power, by themselves, to destroy the open, informal, trust-based culture we need to win today and tomorrow.

Since people are hired for aptitude, but fired or promoted for attitude, are we asking all of the right questions in interviews? What about community involvement? What about personal values? These points

SINCE PEOPLE ARE HIRED FOR APTITUDE, BUT FIRED OR PROMOTED FOR ATTITUDE, ARE WE ASKING ALL OF THE RIGHT QUESTIONS IN INTERVIEWS?

should carry just as much weight as experience and skill when it comes to inviting someone into your corporate family. The practice of developing a resume has historically focused on education and experience. Applicants sometimes put so much emphasis in these two areas, they have little to say, if anything, about their personal values or community involvement. I list my community leadership roles and involvement on my resume ahead of work experience. Because when I'm the one hiring, this is what I want to know first. I figure if someone cares about their broader community, they are going to care about their corporate community just as much.

The practice of interviewing is much the same. We need to ask ourselves if the traditional approach of sitting across from one another in a conference room is the best way to really get to know someone and their values. Think creatively about settings where conversation is better fueled, such as the golf course, a nearby walking trail, or maybe it's as simple as the coffee shop around the corner. After all, you may not have an engagement problem, but instead, a selection problem.

When the Fit is Right

United Parcel Service (UPS) has a long history of high social capital, and over the years has preferred to hire people who *fit* the company's constitution - who share the organization's core values of hard work, cooperation and commitment - over applicants who may be more experienced but lack these social-capital-building traits. This long-standing culture has become synonymous with the UPS brand and customer experience.

Here's an example. My house was one of the last daily stops in my neighborhood for the UPS route; and on one Friday when I needed to leave town early, but needed my package, I looked for the UPS driver in my neighborhood since I knew he had to be somewhere close by. It didn't take long for me to spot the big brown truck. The driver of the truck took one good look at me and said, *You're 117 Carriage Court.* I was shocked. Especially since I'm rarely home when packages are delivered. It was no problem getting my package off of the truck early, and of course no ID was required because he recognized me. What struck me the most, however, was that he proceeded to use our unconventional encounter as an opportunity to ask me if I had been finding my packages okay in the location where he was leaving them.

This same point of people and constitution alignment also reverberates each and every time I need an oil change, and here's why. You could expect that working in a tire shop may not represent the pinnacle of anyone's career, but in fact it is. You haven't met a happier, more enthusiastic bunch unless you've been to Tires, Tires, Tires in Sioux Falls, South Dakota. This crew could not be more excited about helping you pick out the right tires for your vehicle, or simply helping you get your car tuned up for a weekend trip. This translates into the best place to get tires and oil changes in Sioux Falls because of the superior customer experience – even though they sell the same kind of tires as the competitor down the road at the same price. Each time I go there, my heart fills with jealousy at how much fun these guys are having at work – and on a Saturday nonetheless! So while I wait for my car in the cozy waiting area - fireplace, couch, cookies – I begin to daydream. I envision myself behind the counter, working alongside of them, enjoying the camaraderie and laughs that ensue. But that's where the wheels come off (figuratively and literally). I'm quickly reminded that I know nothing about tires. And if I'm completely honest with myself, I am not interested in learning either. As soon as customers figured this out, I would fall flat in my customer service delivery.

Enculturation

> *en·cul·tur·a·tion (noun): The process by which an individual learns the traditional content of a culture and assimilates its practices and values.*

When an organization's constitution is well defined, enculturating new hires into your community fuels not just social capital, but also efficiency. It immediately reinforces to the new employee that he or she is valued and important. When Bob Gett served as CEO of major web-consulting firm Viant, the company believed it took about seven months to fully embed new employees and teach them enough about the company to make them productive. As a result, they had a three-week employee orientation program. Gett said the program was important in creating social capital that served new employees through their entire careers at Viant, while giving them an immediate sense of membership.

A key piece of the enculturation process is ensuring new hires understand the significance of the work they will do for the organization. This may involve having them job shadow the customer experience. One of the most impactful moments in my career was job shadowing a physician-scientist who was assessing a 2-year-old boy with an undiagnosed rare disease. The boy was blind, had limited use of his arms, and it was clear he would most likely never walk. It opened my eyes to how critical the physician's research was in his pursuit to better understand the genomic basis of rare disease, and the devastation it had equally on children and their parents. This experience reinvigorated me as a marketer to build awareness surrounding the significance of the problems this physician could solve with increased exposure with collaborating scientists and more funding for research.

Enculturating new employees is especially important for companies whose people are its products, such as doctors and nurses in the example just offered. Employees must become synonymous with the brand that the organization promises to its customers. In order to achieve brand differentiation, employees (i.e. your constitution and culture) must personify the brand in a consistent and compelling way. In instances like these where people are the product, you can assume if the employees aren't happy, the customer isn't either.

ENCULTURATING NEW EMPLOYEES IS ESPECIALLY IMPORTANT FOR COMPANIES WHOSE PEOPLE ARE ITS PRODUCTS.

According to Gallup, businesses scoring in the top 50 percentile for employee engagement have 86 percent higher customer ratings.

Enculturation occurs during new employee onboarding and orientation, but its staying power is influenced by two key variables. First, how well the organization follows its constitution. And second, how long employees stay with the organization. Of all of the brands I have come into contact with, Midwest grocery chain, Hy-Vee, is one of the best examples of this remarkable staying power, which results in a consistency of culture across the entire organization. Hy-Vee's brand promise of *a helpful smile in every aisle* rings true at every location, in every community, and every state of its operations. Whether you live in Kansas City, Missouri or are traveling through Des Moines, Iowa, your Hy-Vee experience will be the same. If you look lost, someone will offer to help you find what you need. When you approach the meat counter, someone is always there eager to fill your order. When you check out, someone will ask you if you found everything okay. And, when you leave, someone will say *thank you* and *have a nice day.* You might also notice one of the Hy-Vee semis headed down the highway with the names and faces of dedicated employees on the side.

I recently asked a Hy-Vee manager, *How do you guys do it? What's the secret?* He responded by saying there is rarely a meeting with leadership where customer service isn't mentioned, and that people tend to stay with the organization for a long time because they believe in the company.

Internal Communications

Business needs that most often precipitate internal communications planning include reinforcement of the constitution, the desire for increased employee engagement, and/or organizational cohesiveness in how goals are collectively achieved. An effective internal communications plan shows the link between the specific business need and how internal communications is then a possible solution. It is a means to an end, and not an end within itself; and includes goals and objectives that are measurable.

Internal communications is not a process of using official, one-way channels of communication, such as emails, corporate newsletters and intranet articles. Instead, it's embedded in your overall engagement strategy representing constant interactions within the organization that convey meaning and a sense of community. These experiences are then co-created amongst employees, facilitating and nurturing how employees choose to become an extension of the brand. In addition to having a clear constitution, important answers to know include:

1. What are the key aspirations of the organization?
2. What do employees need to feel, think and then do in order to support those aspirations?
3. Where are employees' perceptions now?
4. What needs to change that will inspire employees to join in contributing to and celebrating those aspirations?

The word *brand* is too often confused with the way in which marketing and public relations tactics are executed. Your brand is what is happening inside the walls of the organization. It's what you do, why you do it, and how you collectively get it done. It is the core of your constitution. This is why the internal communications team alone cannot fix gaps that exist between what an organization is and how its employees and customers feel. Here is another way of saying it. If you are not first meeting your employee promise, you cannot meet your brand promise to customers – because every employee serves either the customer or supports another employee in serving the customer. The employee promise goes beyond compensation as noted in Chapter 2. More importantly, it's about integrity; as we just discussed, walking the talk. Integrity is doing what you say you are going to do, and how well you follow your constitution. Employees, or customers for that matter, will not become loyal to an organization that lacks integrity. If you have to tell your employees to become brand ambassadors, or offer incentives for them to do so, then: 1) You aren't following your constitution; or 2) Your constitution isn't worth believing in.

When Gallup surveyed a random sampling of 3,000 employees, less than half felt they knew what their company stood for and what made their company's brand different from competitors. Not only do we want our employees to serve as an authentic extension of the brand when they interact with customers, we

> **BRAND DIFFERENTIATION AND THE EVERYONE-BELONGS-TO-THE-MARKETING-DEPARTMENT CONCEPT ARE TWO GREAT REASONS FOR ORGANIZATIONS TO DEVELOP AND RESOURCE AN EMPLOYEE ENGAGEMENT STRATEGY.**

want them to do the same in our communities and protect the brand. When organizations like Hy-Vee, Tires, Tires, Tires and UPS achieve this kind of brand authenticity and ambassadorship, they need little if any marketing to remain competitive in their industry. The customer experience (or customer delight) translates into customer loyalty, which translates once more to customer evangelism. Brand differentiation and the everyone-belongs-to-the-Marketing-Department concept are two great reasons for organizations to develop and resource an employee engagement strategy.

Step 2 - Ensure the work of the organization serves a higher purpose.

Corporate philanthropy is present in a variety of shapes and sizes, including direct cash contributions, foundation grants, stock donations, employee time, product donations and other in-kind gifts. Some corporations have developed creative strategies to engage their customers in giving. Crate and Barrel is one of them. Since 2006, the company has given its customers thank you gift cards to DonorsChoose.org, an online charity that connects donors to classrooms in need. The gift cards empowered customers to allocate Crate and Barrel's contributions to classrooms across the nation based on educational projects and programs submitted by teachers. This strategy has funded 14,500 projects, benefited 347,000 students, and cultivated an additional 36,500 new DonorsChoose.org donors as the result of Crate and Barrel introducing their customers to the website. On average, Crate and Barrel customers gave $.40 for every $1 redeemed by the gift cards.

Quality of Corporate Philanthropy

A group of CEOs was concerned about the level, and more importantly quality, of corporate philanthropy, so it formed the Committee on Encouraging Corporate Philanthropy (CECP) in 1999 to tackle the issue. According to CECP member Sidney Taurel, Chairman of Eli Lilly and Company, "Like all companies, Lilly has a contract with society. Part of that contract is embedded in laws, and part of the tacit understanding that as we fulfill our responsibilities to society, society will allow us the freedom to operate."

CECP conducted a survey of corporate executives from around the world and found that 84 percent believe that society now expects businesses to take a much more active role in environmental, social, and political issues than it did five years ago. Fewer than 20 percent said their company was very or extremely effective in meeting social or business goals with their philanthropy.

CECPs efforts focus largely on moving corporate America away from *check writing* toward leadership, collaboration and global efforts. They have developed a framework that includes procedures for assessing whether or not corporate giving achieves the intended outcome as well as procedures for determining an overall social return on investment.

CECP also promotes a core business strategy, called Sustainable Value Creation, focused on addressing societal issues by identifying new opportunities for competitive advantage that simultaneously builds profits and community benefit. An example is in rural Mexico, where PepsiCo faced business constriction because of low-quality local corn. PepsiCo leadership identified where the pitfalls were – the skills of local providers and an inadequate farming and transportation infrastructure. Subsequently, PepsiCo developed and implemented a plan that contributed to the overall development of low-income farming families through technical and business training, transfers of technology, and farming contracts. This reduced costs and improved the quality of the corn, which raised the community's standard of living. Sustainable value creation: Helping business and people at the same time.

Philanthropy and Higher Purpose

Corporate social responsibility (CSR) and philanthropy is certainly already taking place on a widespread basis; however, building it into your corporate brand and culture allows social capital to build both inside and outside the walls of an organization. It adds fuel to the organization's higher purpose. Corporations should leverage philanthropy as an authentic extension of who they are as a brand. It can't appear to be done out of obligation, but instead something consistent with the company's mission and constitution. In other words, do not

> **CORPORATIONS SHOULD LEVERAGE PHILANTHROPY AS AN AUTHENTIC EXTENSION OF WHO THEY ARE AS A BRAND.**

put lipstick on a pig in pursuit of public relations value.

International pharmaceutical company Novo Nordisk could not be more authentic. Novo Nordisk, a leading insulin manufacturer, understands that access to pharmaceutical products is only half of the equation when it comes to improved health outcomes for people living with diabetes. As a result, Novo Nordisk leadership has dedicated the company's overall focus toward helping people overcome diabetes, versus only marketing and selling insulin to health care organizations. One example is how the company has adopted the Rosebud Indian Reservation in South Dakota. Rosebud represents one of the poorest communities in the nation as well as one of the highest for diabetes prevalence. In addition to building a new community recreation center in Rosebud, Novo Nordisk also implements an annual Keep Rosebud Warm clothing drive across its organization every fall to provide Rosebud residents with warm hats, gloves, mittens and socks.

Here's an article that ran in the Todd County Tribune capturing the extraordinary extension of the Novo Nordisk brand and higher purpose:

Rosebud Sioux Tribe Diabetes Prevention breaks ground for Wellness Center
March 14, 2013, by Rich Winter

Rosebud Sioux Tribe (RST) Diabetes Prevention Director Connie Brushbreaker received a most curious call in October of 2010 during a drive to Kansas to visit her daughter Laura. On the other end of the line was a representative from a company called Novo Nordisk, Inc. and as Brushbreaker moved through the initial introductions, she could hardly believe the words she was hearing from a complete stranger. "We are a major world-wide pharmaceutical company and we've been observing the RST Diabetes

Prevention Center for some time and we'd like to help you build a new Wellness Center," the voice on the other end of the line told Brushbreaker.

The ensuing conversation went something like this.
"Who's going to fund it?" asked Brushbreaker.
"We are," said the voice on the other end of the line.
"You're kidding, right?" asked Brushbreaker.

The 2010 phone call was no joke and Brushbreaker, representatives from Novo Nordisk and J. Scull Construction gathered Friday to break ground for the new Wellness Center that is expected to be finished by early August of 2013. "Novo Nordisk makes decisions to do things like this that are intrinsic to the needs of a community," Ken Inchausti Director of Media Relations for Novo Nordisk said of his company's investment.

Novo Nordisk learned of the Rosebud Reservation and the prevalent nature of the diabetes that runs rampant here from a group of physicians that worked at the Rosebud IHS hospital and the diabetes prevention program run by the tribe that had correspondence with Novo Nordisk. After learning what the conditions were like here, the company having never built a facility like this in the United States, felt like the Wellness Center was a must.

"What can we do to make a difference in the community," was the resounding and singular voice from a company that is one of the largest diabetes pharmaceutical companies in the world, said Inchausti. The new Wellness Center is expected to be nearly 13-thousand square feet, complete with a functioning teaching kitchen, a physician's office, two workout spaces, one consolidated area for weight lifting along with multiple offices for the Diabetes Prevention Center Employees.

In addition, Novo Nordisk is helping with the purchase of a mobile unit that Brushbreaker likens to that of the Wic Mobile Unit. "The mobile unit is going to be administered by Health Administration of the Rosebud Sioux Tribe," Brushbreaker said. "It gives us a chance to take our facilities, our testing and our message to the farthest reaches of our reservation."

Inchausti insists that Novo Nordisk is not just coming in to provide a facility and then leave. "We are looking at this as a pilot program and we need to see how this works," Inchausti said. "We want to make the right commitment with the infrastructure and the support, and be there to ensure that this facility is up and running."

For Brushbreaker, the issue of diabetes is very serious, and one that is most personal. Diagnosed with the disease fifteen years ago, Brushbreaker has seen her parents both go through dialysis. "It was very hard to see their pain and also the limitations that diabetes put on their lives," Brushbreaker said. The birth of her first grand-daughter this year now makes her own personal battle with weight and her own struggle with diabetes, the most important battle she says she'll face. "I don't want any of my kids to see me on dialysis and I want to be around for as long as I can to spend time with that grand-baby," Brushbreaker said.

Novo Nordisk founded the World Diabetes Foundation to save the lives of those affected by diabetes in developing countries. The Foundation supported a United Nations resolution to fight diabetes, making diabetes the only other disease alongside of HIV/AIDS to have a commitment to combat at a United Nations level.

When talking about the organization's mission, I recently heard a Novo Nordisk leader state, "...you could say the mission of our company is to put ourselves out of business. We do not want people to have a need for insulin anymore. Ultimately, we want diabetes to go away." Novo Nordisk has been ranked several times as one of Fortune's top 100 companies to work for.

Organizations with a clear sense of higher purpose will hold a distinct and prevailing advantage over the next decade. Statistics show that as soon as 2015, the majority of our workforce will be comprised of Gen Y, also referred to as Millennials. And by 2025, Millennials will make up 75 percent of the world's workforce. When surveyed, Millennials indicate higher purpose is a key variable, if not one of the most important variables, in choosing where to work and where to buy. From a recruitment and marketing perspective, with a meaningful higher purpose, Millennials are motivated to work for you and buy from you.

Philanthropic Consumerism

Philanthropy-focused corporations could completely transform the way consumers consume in America. The decision is ours as consumers with an increasing number of product choices offering a direct tie to philanthropy. For example, take the 30-years-and-growing Newman's Own food line. According to the Newman's Own website:

> Paul Newman was committed to helping make the world a better place. To carry on his philanthropic legacy, Newman's Own Foundation donates all net royalties and profits after taxes it receives from the sale of Newman's Own products to charities worldwide.

Santa Monica-based TOMS Shoes was started with charity in mind. For every pair of TOMS shoes sold, TOMS gives a pair to a child in need. TOMS stands for *tomorrow's*. The program is called One for One. TOMS founder Blake Mycoskie explained:

> I thought, well, what if you had a situation where you could create a business instead of a charity? Where for every pair of shoes you sold you gave one away. That way, you had something you could continue and sustain. I was really into this idea of sustainability... that way when the kids' feet grew or the shoe wore out, it would become our way to continue to give them new ones, as well as allow our customers to continue to participate in the movement. So instead of a charity, I started a business encompassing a one-for-one model where you buy a pair and we give a pair. Very simple. Totally transparent.

TOMS shoes have become popular across America, not only because of their style or comfort, but because of what they represent. To the degree even that other traditional shoe brands have copied *both* the TOMS look *and* donation strategy. Freewaters shoes is a similar concept as TOMS, where proceeds are instead directed toward providing clean water to those in need. Consumers feel better knowing they

PHILANTHROPY-FOCUSED CORPORATIONS COULD COMPLETELY TRANSFORM THE WAY CONSUMERS CONSUME IN AMERICA.

are giving back. Mycoskie has since expanded this sustainable model to eye wear, providing glasses to children in need across the globe. What will Mycoskie come up with next?

Starbucks has offered Fairtrade coffee since 2000, and has become one of the largest purchasers of Fairtrade-certified coffee in the world. They say not only does it meet their customers' expectations, but helps protect the environment and the livelihood of farmers in coffee-growing regions.

And perhaps least expected of all brands is Rolex. The truth is, philanthropy is a significant undercurrent of the Rolex legacy. Hans Wilsdorf, the entrepreneur behind the Rolex watch, was orphaned at the age of 12 in Geneva, Switzerland. When his wife passed away in 1944, Wilsdorf established the Hans Wilsdorf Foundation in which he left all of his Rolex shares, making sure that a large percentage of the company's income would always go to charity. The company is still owned by a private trust and the foundation directs a meaningful portion of its Rolex profits to children's initiatives, entrepreneurial innovation and cultural endeavors.

Many corporations have creatively aligned themselves with a cause important to their organization by very simply offering consumers a choice of participating in a movement through product color. Apple is an example, where they offer the red iPod, where proceeds go toward Product Red, started by U2's Bono to end AIDS in Africa.

Ideological Clarity

Granted, not every corporation can be built square on the foundation of philanthropy, but the lesson about the importance of ideological clarity was perhaps best played out in the movie *Company Men*. GTX Corporation CEO, played by Craig T. Nelson, laid off employees in droves as a continued measure to improve profit margins while he remained the 19th highest paid CEO in the nation. He was also adamant not to sell the company's new penthouse corporate offices to reduce expenses and thwart the number of employees affected. Long-time GTX executive, played by Tommy Lee Jones, had been with the CEO from the beginning and helped build the company from the ground up. His leadership and years of dedication to the company weren't enough to save him, and he became the last casualty of downsizing. The movie closes with Tommy Lee Jones working to start a new company built upon GTX's historic mission and principles. He hires back former GTX employees to capture the relationships, tacit knowledge, and belief of purpose they once had in GTX at an earlier time. More importantly, the movie is a classic tale - and today what has become a common tale - of how lives are both quickly and easily turned upside down when the sense of corporate community and purpose is lost.

Businesses and products are developed everyday because there are entrepreneurs who feel the product or service is needed to improve our quality of life for many different important reasons. They are passionate and driven to bring them to market because of how they can help others. John Seely Brown who oversaw research for two decades at Xerox Park once said, "The job of leadership today is not just to make money, it's to make meaning." He went on to say that this is what people seek in their employment. "Talented people are looking for organizations that offer not only money, but spiritual goals that energize, that resonate with the personal values of the people who work there, the kind of mission that offers people a chance to do work that makes a difference."

This perspective has been taught in other popular leadership and management literature as well, including *Conscious Capitalism* and *Built to Last*. The message in Jim Collins' *Built to Last* was that values and

> **STARTING OUT WITH IDEOLOGICAL CLARITY MATTERS EVEN MORE THAN HOW GOOD OR BAD THE ORIGINAL PRODUCT OR SERVICE IS.**

a clear sense of purpose were the key ingredients to organizational success. The authors said their research for the book confirmed that starting out with ideological clarity matters even more than how good or bad the original product or service is.

When organizations have ideological clarity they are able to engage the right people, people who can believe in the same purpose and values as the CEO; not because he or she has positional power, but because the purpose and values of the work are worth believing in – like ending diabetes. They follow the leader as if they are disciples of his or her cause. In addition to those already mentioned, familiar brands that have done this successfully include The Container Store, Patagonia, Google, Panera Bread, Southwest Airlines, Costco, and REI, to name a few. If it's positional power alone that moves the gears of an organization, the engine will inevitably grind to a halt and need to be replaced.

CITIZENS AT WORK

Step 3 - Make the workplace a platform for civic engagement and education.

Corporate executives have the unique opportunity to make the workplace a platform for civic involvement and education. In one private-sector organization where I ran the marketing and planning division, we brought in all the candidates for local office prior to the fall election in the company's auditorium. City council, county commissioners, state offices, you name it. Each candidate was given a specified amount of time to talk about their platform, with time following for open Q and A from employees. As corporate leaders, this took us one step beyond simply encouraging employees to vote, but we played an important role in ensuring an educated vote.

Encouraging Civic Education and Leadership

Chances are a good number of your employees do not know who is on the school board, who their city council representative is, and even more do not know their county commissioner. These are the people deciding the quality of education our children will receive, how much we will pay in property taxes, and how well our local roads and bridges are maintained and cared for.

CHANCES ARE A GOOD NUMBER OF YOUR EMPLOYEES DO NOT KNOW WHO IS ON THE SCHOOL BOARD, WHO THEIR CITY COUNCIL REPRESENTATIVE IS, AND EVEN MORE DO NOT KNOW THEIR COUNTY COMMISSIONER.

Involvement in community life, such as public meetings, has declined by 35 percent over the last 25 years. Public conversations are inherent to solving challenges our society is facing. Social policy expert John McKnight says the most sustainable improvements in community occur when citizens discover their own power to act. Whatever the issue – the environment, crime, unemployment, guns, literacy – it is when citizens stop relying on government as the only solution, and realize they have the ability to shape and influence community outcomes, that things really happen.

Here is part of the problem. As community-building author Peter Block states, we have put elected officials in a difficult role. We relate to them as if we are consumers, not citizens. We want them to solve for us those issues that we should be solving for ourselves. In his book, *Community: The structure of belonging,* he talks about the unique yet underutilized opportunity elected officials have as conveners of social capital in the public sector:

> The customer model, in which elected officials exist to satisfy citizen demands, is a disservice to community, even though citizens love it. Elected officials are partners

with citizens, not suppliers. The most useful role that elected officials can perform is to bring citizens together. They have this convening capacity like no one else in a city, but it is way underutilized. If elected officials take on this role as their primary one, we may still occasionally request that they pass some legislation or ordinance that serves us, but this should be the exception. If we continue to define elected officials primarily as legislators, then we are going to have to endure the results of their productivity.

Another paradox we have placed on elected officials is their dual role of civic representation and business savvy. Everyone wants or expects government to run like business; however, when we hold elections, candidates aren't required to have an MBA or any business operational experience for that matter. Consequently, elected officials quickly find themselves in positions where they are making multi-million-dollar decisions with little budgeting or administration background.

Perhaps more important than using the workplace to nourish public conversation and further an educated vote, workplace candidate forums expose business professionals to the role of public office, and encourages them to step forward and provide public sector leadership. It exposes them to the reality that they are the community, and if they want a higher standard for their community, they need to be a part of the solution. Using the workplace as a platform to cultivate civic engagement is the best way to inspire a new generation of elected officials who start and lead public conversations, mobilizing communities around problem solving rather than just votes.

Responsibility to Community

Consider creating incentives for your workforce in community involvement. Actually, don't consider it, this is your responsibility. Here is what I mean. In a Midwest-based corporation, an email went out encouraging employ-

IN 2011, ONLY ONE IN FOUR ADULTS VOLUNTEERED IN THE UNITED STATES.

ees to help sandbag for a pending flood in a sister city where the organization had a large corporate office and several retail service centers. While the email encouraged employees to take guilt-free time away from work to reinforce the flood efforts, it also reminded employees to use their PTO.

The flood example demonstrates how leaders see their business as separate from community. They do not see their employees and community as one of the same. If our private sector does not feel a strong sense of community responsibility, then who are we relying on? Our government and nonprofit sectors. Wait a minute. That's still us. Your employees are the ones paying taxes and making charitable donations. When an office or department holds a United Way rally, it isn't raising money for a mysterious group of people living outside the walls of the organization. They are raising money for one another. As the United Way's Laura Bowman stated in this book's Forward, "We are all interconnected, and we all have skin in the game."

In 2011, only one in four adults volunteered in the United States. Corporations with diverse volunteer programs that reflect employee values are authentically bringing community into the workplace. Even better are executives who lead by example and actively volunteer in a cause they are personally passionate about. Here are some examples of organizations that align both volunteer time and employee donations with corporate giving:

- Microsoft is one of the largest corporate donors in the world. Microsoft has donated more than $1 billion through the company's employee giving programs. In 2005, Microsoft instituted a Dollars for Doers Program where the company provides $17 grants for every hour a Microsoft employee volunteers. Microsoft also matches each employee's nonprofit donations up to $12,000 per year.

  After national and global catastrophic events, when employees arrive to work and turn on their computer, an automatic prompt appears along with a convenient button encouraging employees to donate and reminding them that Microsoft will match their contribution. I recently heard a Microsoft leader state, "This makes it hard not to feel compelled to contribute, knowing my employer is at the ready to double my money." She also mentioned how motivated she is to get hours in volunteering in the concession stand or ticket booth at her daughter's school to maximize Microsoft's contribution for her time.

- ExxonMobil offers an employee matching gift program by providing 3:1 matches to educational institutions and 1:1 matches to other eligible organizations. For every 20 hours an employee volunteers, the company will provide a $500 grant to the nonprofit ($25 per hour volunteered). The company provides up to $2,000 in volunteer grants per employee each year.

- Through Verizon's Volunteer Incentive Program (VIP), the company provides volunteer grants to organizations where employees volunteer on a regular basis. After employees volunteer for 50 hours in a year, the company provides a $750 grant to the organization ($15 per hour). The company also matches employee donations to schools up to $5,000 annually and $1,000 to all other 501(c)(3) organizations annually.

- Coinstar/Redbox has one of the lowest volunteer thresholds before an employee is eligible to request a match. There are four different volunteer grant levels (all come to $15 per volunteer hour): 10 hours > $150 grant; 20 hours > $300 grant; 30 hours > $450 grant; and 40 hours > $600 grant. Coinstar also offers a matching gift program where the company matches employee donations up to $2,000 annually.

Of Fortune 500 companies, 65 percent offer matching gift programs and 40 percent offer volunteer grant programs. Programs like these not only incent community involvement, but also empower each employee to feel like they have access to the corporate giving pot. Additionally, many organizations, such as Oklahoma's family-owned First Bethany Bank and Trust N.A., also consider volunteer hours as a factor in employee reviews.

Volunteer PTO

Recognizing our society's dilemma today of *not enough time*, another widely used option is to simply give paid time off (PTO) for civic involvement and volunteering. Corporations, including Timberland, Brinks, Hasbro, Stride Rite, and Sony Music, all have policies allowing employees to take time off *with pay* to volunteer. According to social enterprise researcher, James Austin, community service is a form of job enrichment that

A GROWING NUMBER OF STUDIES CONFIRM VOLUNTEER PROGRAMS SIGNIFICANTLY INCREASE EMPLOYEE MORALE, LOYALTY AND PRODUCTIVITY.

provides psychic income and a greater sense of fulfillment. Austin points to a growing number of studies that confirm volunteer programs significantly increase employee morale, loyalty and productivity.

In practice, however, encouraging volunteerism across an organization is not as easy as it sounds. Research has revealed a problem area. The findings show both top management and line employees seem to be eager and readily mobilized, however middle management is the sticking ground as they face tremendous pressures from above to meet sales or performance targets and are often stretched on resources. These demands make them see community service activities as a drain on their scarce resources and their resistance creates mixed messages.

There is a vast existence of corporate volunteer programs, but it's difficult to tell how truly embedded and supported they are in organizational culture. If expectations surrounding community service are commensurate with sales and performance targets, then employees of all ranks will feel both responsible and emboldened to be successful at both. Accomplishments on both fronts should be lifted up as wins in the eyes of the company. One doesn't need to come at the expense of the other.

Step 4 - Create transparency and community gathering spaces.

My years working in the public sector reinforced this tenet: Do not become friends with those you work with. After all, you might have to discipline, or heaven forbid, fire someone. Bottom line: A cold work environment = a fair work environment.

So this is the foundation that we want to build work relationships on – on the assumption that the employee

STRATEGIES THAT BUILD TRANSPARENCY AND RELATIONSHIPS BETWEEN COLLEAGUES PERPETUATE A MORE COMMUNITY-ORIENTED WORK ENVIRONMENT.

might disappoint us? Shockingly, Step 4 turns this assumption on its head. Embracing the idea that work and one's personal life need not always be kept separate (again, we spend the majority of our waking hours at work) allows the workplace to function in a more humane way. Finding strategies that build transparency and relationships between colleagues is what perpetuates a more community-oriented work environment – a work environment that cultivates trust, respect, accountability and open communication. A work environment that regards employees as people over professionals. A work environment that employees do not mind going to every day.

When levels of trust are high, team members speak more freely with one another. They become more genuine in their interactions and how they approach their work together. They become more efficient. In a high-trust environment, you will hear statements such as, *I made a mistake and I need your help.* Or, *You always have great ideas around this sort of thing, what do you think?* Egos and maneuvering get stuck on the sidelines and team members who have bonded together through trusting relationships get the real work done.

Corporate Libraries and Parks

An example of creating workplace transparency can be found at Minneapolis-based Red Brick Health, an organization that administers workplace wellness programs for many Fortune 500 corporations. At Red Brick you'll find pictures of employees, from the executive office to line staff, on display along with images that represent their personal interests, such as hobbies, talents, favorite quotes, and family life, as well as information about their current company projects. And talk about ideological clarity, this dedicated bunch wears their running clothes to work so they can get five miles in over the lunch hour or during an afternoon break.

Just like communities have libraries and parks to promote and enhance community culture, corporations need the same. These corporate libraries and parks can be as simple as a conference table placed in the middle of cubeland that offers a common gathering place for lunch; or a comfortable room with

> **JUST LIKE COMMUNITIES HAVE LIBRARIES AND PARKS TO PROMOTE AND ENHANCE COMMUNITY CULTURE, CORPORATIONS NEED THE SAME.**

a fireplace, deck, snacks and an oven to bake chocolate chip cookies – referred to as *Zen Café* at marketing agency Sundog Interactive. Red Brick Health has a ping pong room. Spaces such as these nourish conversation, encourage collaboration and create a strong sense of community. Remember in Step 1 – *I don't trust anyone I work with?*

Lars Kolind, former CEO of hearing-aid giant Oticon, noticed employees who met each other on the stairways often engaged in conversation. He subsequently built broader stairwell landings with coffee machines and places to sit down that would encourage employees to extend their already-existing conversations.

When I toured Lakeville, Minnesota (a Twin Cities suburb) Police Department's new facility, they had purposely built only one coffee area and placed it in the middle of the police station. In this example, Police Chief Tom Vonhof said the reason wasn't necessarily to get people chatting for purposes of morale, but instead, to solve crimes. And it worked.

Here's another example. After merging with Fargo-based MeritCare, Sanford Health, located in Sioux Falls, South Dakota, initiated a daily bus route running between both cities (3.5 hours distance), not only giving employees the opportunity to have face-to-face meetings with their new colleagues, but also allowing staff time on the bus to engage in conversations and get to know one another. This is an example where Sanford Health CEO Kelby Krabbenhoft chose a high-touch, low-tech option during a key milestone transition for both organizations. It was an important aspect of bringing together two distinct organizational cultures. Ancillary benefits of the bus were that it offered employees a comfortable and productive environment for travel, including snacks, beverages and a wireless network.

Caution: *Us versus them*

When it comes to space, however, proceed with caution. Space can often show physical separation between leaders and employees, creating an *us versus them* environment. These physical separations tend to occur through executive floors and suites, executive dining rooms, and even furniture selections. To avoid this separation, Zappos CEO Tony Hsieh decided having his cube positioned right in the middle of everyone else's at company headquarters made the most sense for his leadership style and the organization's constitution. Perhaps its value #10 at play again – *Be Humble.*

In some companies, particularly corporations that cover a large geographic footprint, it is more practical and efficient to co-locate the executive cabinet in one central location. However, again, this is where our work continues as leaders. Leaders must be intentional about removing perceived separations. Visibility can manifest in many ways other than location of office space, such as informal office walk-abouts or attending workplace events and gatherings where you know your employees will be present.

MANAGEMENT DESIGNED TO ENGAGE

Step 5 - Invest in first-line leaders.

We need to shift the way we think about how the gears of an organization operate. What is usually the first thing an organization cuts when it runs into budget troubles? Training and employee development. Who typically gets the high-end perks, such as premier parking or home-plate tickets? The C-Suite. You can see where this is going and it's time to start thinking about how middle management fits strategically with what gets done day to day.

The Supervisor/Employee Relationship

When Gallup conducted a survey of over 80,000 employees, it learned the number-one driver of engagement is an employee's relationship with their supervisor. A 2009 Sirota Intelligence Study also revealed that disengaged managers are *three times* more likely to have disengaged employees. McGill University management expert Henry Mintzberg suggests, "Perhaps it's time to rebuild companies not from the top down or even the bottom up, but from the middle out – through groups of middle managers who bond together and drive key changes in their organization."

> **THE NUMBER-ONE DRIVER OF ENGAGEMENT IS AN EMPLOYEE'S RELATIONSHIP WITH THEIR SUPERVISOR.**

If we're going to follow Mintzberg's advice, then we need to start focusing more on the group of people who are charged with providing the lion's share of day-to-day leadership to the rest of the organization. We also need to take into consideration the generational changes that will occur in management ranks over the next decade. As baby boomers retire, much younger and less experienced Gen X and Y leaders will take their place. Management development and engagement will be become more critical than ever before. Organizations that effectively train and develop this group of young leaders will lead the way in building social capital.

Charging Management's Batteries

In every organization where I have worked, public and private, there is a similar practice of bringing together the executive team on a regular basis, typically monthly, for corporate updates and to discuss organizational challenges and opportunities. The CEO gives the update and leads the discussion. But seldom is this same practice implemented with middle management. Isn't it just as important for middle managers (again, this is the group providing the lion's share of day-to-day leadership to the organization) to hear vision and goals directly from the CEO, as well as participate in multidisciplinary discussion and shared learning with peers? Not doing this reinforces that only the executive cabinet is good enough. Doing it ensures middle management's batteries are fully charged for mobilization.

Here is something else to consider as we think about middle management. Many employees indicate they feel their job doesn't allow them to work to their full potential. They feel underutilized. They feel they could be helping more with strategy and not buried in the *muck* of day-to-day operations. What your employees feel versus what is reality remains to be seen. What can be seen clearly, however, is that day-to-day operations are hard. Muck is difficult to walk through. It takes an extremely talented and experienced person (someone who has walked through the muck for a while and in different places) to keep budgets in alignment, meet operational goals and lead an engaged workforce.

To some degree, it may be human nature that tells all of us we're actually better than what we are. How many of us haven't made one of the following two statements in our career? *I could do her job so much better... If I was just given the opportunity, I could make some real changes around here.* There aren't enough executive positions to go around to satisfy this appetite. There are only so many CEOs, COOs and VPs needed to run an organization.

So what do we do with those who get left behind from the C-Suite? What do we do with those who feel their potential exceeds their current role? We make sure they do not leave. We engage them. After all, they might be right! We stop making them feel like they're only good enough to walk through the muck. We tell them, and more importantly show them, we need them for much more. Our hard work as leaders continues.

Motivation and Autonomy

Daniel Pink, who has researched the science behind motivation, tells us exactly how to engage middle management.

He is calling for a renaissance of *self direction*, rather than better management; and says the heart of empowerment is in having autonomy and no longer seeing employees as pawns, but instead players. According to Pink, the opposite of autonomy is control. And since they sit at different poles of the behavioral compass, they point us toward different destinations: "Control leads to compliance; autonomy leads to engagement."

A sense of autonomy promotes higher productivity, less burnout and increased levels of psychological well-being. In his book *Drive: The surprising truth about what motivates us*, Pink offers the four T's of autonomy: Task (what people do), Time (when they do it), Technique (how they do it), and Team (whom they do it with). He uses the example of Atlassian software executive Mike Cannon-Brookes who wanted to spark creativity amongst his team. He

> A SENSE OF AUTONOMY PROMOTES HIGHER PRODUCTIVITY, LESS BURNOUT AND INCREASED LEVELS OF PSYCHOLOGICAL WELL-BEING.

decided to encourage them to spend a day working on any problem they wanted, even if it wasn't part of their regular job. What he found was the day gave birth to ideas for new products and improvements on existing ones. So Cannon-Brookes decided to make this practice of autonomy a permanent part of the Atlassian culture. He says, "If you don't pay enough, you can lose people. But beyond that, money is not a motivator. What matters are these other features."

Full Rights to the Four T's

As a leader, ask yourself if you give your managers full rights to the four T's. When is the last time your COO, VP, director or manager made a key hire, and you interjected yourself into the hiring process? Maybe you told him or her who you thought they should hire or what their structure for getting the work done should look like. Or maybe you used your positional power to make the hire yourself and created the structure on your own.

Staying focused on outcomes and staying out of the detail isn't always an easy thing to do as leaders. When is the last time you communicated an important project, and then went on to tell your subordinate exactly how you wanted him or her to get it done? There are a lot of ways to get from point A to point B. We're human, so we're all going to do it slightly different. Sometimes one way is better than another, but not always.

The key point here is, at the end of the day, employees need to know they are accountable to specific performance outcomes. If they know what these outcomes are, and you give your staff full autonomy to meet them, you can hold your staff accountable. Employees then cannot lean on excuses of having a poor team, poor structure, or being forced to use a poor process. However, if you are controlling your employees by choosing their team members for them, or requiring them to use your structure or process, it becomes increasingly difficult for you to hold them accountable. Because now you hold a significant piece of the accountability too.

Step 6 – Create and maintain a line of sight.

Employees have an increased sense of belonging and purpose when they know where they are going. We're not talking about a quick-and-dirty strategic planning session and goal setting; we're talking about knowing exactly where the organization is today, where it needs to be in the future for success, and how I as an individual player contribute to that success. Employee engagement expert Bob Kelleher refers to this as an employee's line of sight.

Macro-level Messaging

When creating a line of sight at the macro level, organizations that only focus on a message of growth are missing the mark. Let's use health care as an example since we're living in an environment where the health care landscape is significantly changing. Why is growth important? Is it for the sake of getting larger (empire building)? Is it larger profits and salaries? Or is it because as a larger company we are stronger, and can afford more clinics, innovative technology and research, which translates into an increased number of community members with access to advanced health care? *This* is the higher purpose.

Organizational goals cannot be solely tied to growth and profits. A book mentioned earlier, *Conscious Capitalism*, makes this important point:

> Profits are an essential and desirable outcome
> for business. Indeed, it is socially irresponsible
> to run a business that does not consistently gen-
> erate profits. Profitable companies can grow

and continue to fulfill their higher purposes, and their profits fuel the growth and progress for our society…Just as happiness is best experienced by not aiming for it directly, profits are best achieved by not making them the primary goals of the business. They are the outcome when companies do business with a sense of higher purpose, build their business on love and caring instead of fear and stress…

Many well-intentioned organizations with a meaningful higher purpose miss the mark on messaging. They miss the mark on communicating their higher purpose. Often times you see it in the public sector after tax dollars have been invested in a new facility or large project. You hear more about the *features*, rather than *benefits*, of how our tax dollars were used. An example of *features* is five new courtrooms and 200 additional jail beds. The *benefit* (or higher purpose) to citizens is that community safety has increased significantly because now the courtrooms are secure and the jail can be more safely managed because it is no longer crowded.

> **MANY WELL-INTENTIONED ORGANIZATIONS WITH A MEANINGFUL HIGHER PURPOSE MISS THE MARK ON MESSAGING.**

Progress and Mastery

On the micro level, a recent multi-year study tracked day-to-day activities, emotions and motivational levels of hundreds of workers in a variety of workplace settings. What really motivates workers? Five workplace factors were considered, including recognition, incentives, interpersonal support, support for making progress and clear goals. The 600 or so managers who responded to the survey said they thought their employees would rank *recognition for good work* as number one. They were

ON DAYS WHEN WORKERS FEEL AS THOUGH THEY ARE MAKING PROGRESS, THEY ARE MOST MOTIVATED.

wrong. In fact, that's what the survey respondents ranked as dead last. The survey revealed, on days when workers feel as though they are *making progress*, they are most motivated.

Identifying meaningful outcomes at the micro level isn't easy either - take local government where employees process driver's licenses day in and day out, or deliver services to people with disabilities. How do you define goals? What is the definition of success? What is the definition of a good day? The message here is take the time to define success as a work unit so it's clear to employees when they are making progress. Knowing you are making progress is necessary for each individual player to feel his or her contribution to overall organizational success.

In addition to progress as a cornerstone to motivation, Pink talks about the importance of *mastery*. He defines mastery as the desire to get better and better at something that matters. He points to research that indicates the highest, most satisfying experiences in people's lives are when goals are clear "...you have to reach the top of the mountain, hit the ball across the net, or mold the clay just right."

Most importantly, the only way to determine if you've mastered something is if you can measure it. And we already know that what gets measured gets managed. Not management through control, but instead through clear and measurable goals. When I was recently at a McDonalds in Superior, Wisconsin, I could see a white board near the drive-through window with *Shift Goals* written at the top, six metrics listed, and hash marks below the metrics. The shift team was keeping track of how well they were meeting each metric; knowing that each of these six metrics collectively leads to the overall desired outcome of a satisfied customer.

Often times you hear overwhelmed managers say, *Not everything can be a priority.* In reality, everything *can* be a priority when each individual team member clearly knows which pieces they are responsible for. Much like the assembly line at Ford, you do not see cars come off the production line without a rear view mirror, a turning signal or air bags. In every workplace, everyone has a role in ensuring the final product or service reaches the showroom at the desired state.

Communicate organizational progress and re-visit these micro-level measurements of success on a regular basis, so employees have a line of sight, not just in their work unit, but also so they understand how they contribute to the larger goals of the organization.

Communication and Coming Together

A common mistake made by managers is not maintaining regularly scheduled team or department meetings. They often fall to the wayside when things get busy. When schedules become full, they get de-prioritized, rescheduled, and ultimately our most reliable channel of communication becomes unreliable.

Physically coming together as an entire department with the department's top executive leadership is central to creating and maintaining a line of sight across both micro and macro levels. It affirms, *You are important and so is your work to the rest of the organization.*

Over-communication is essential to maintaining a line of sight while also affirming an organization's constitution. People are more likely to internalize a message if they hear it with repetition and over a period of time. (Remember the Hy-Vee example of staff meetings and the consistent message surrounding customer service?). If you're saying to yourself, *My schedule is hectic enough as it is. I just don't have time for a bunch of staff meetings*, ask yourself this: *How much time do I spend trying to solve problems that are caused by poor communication?* Poor communication is almost always at the top of the list as a reason why employees lose trust in an organization.

> **OVER-COMMUNICATION IS ESSENTIAL TO MAINTAINING A LINE OF SIGHT WHILE ALSO AFFIRMING AN ORGANIZATION'S CONSTITUTION.**

In addition to the benefits of over-communication - when people come together as a team for any reason - energy, appreciation and an immediate sense of belonging is created and felt by everyone around the table. This is a simple, uncomplicated ingredient for building workplace social capital.

Step 7 - Ensure meaningful feedback mechanisms.

How many organizations still have performance evaluations where you get a 1 or a 2 if you aren't doing your job very well; a 3 if you fairly consistently meet expectations; and a 4 or 5 if you're always spot on, and sometimes flat-out, over-the-top fantastic at what you do? How many supervisors hate administering these performance evaluations on an annual basis? A lot. How many employees hate receiving them? Even more.

The Annual Ritual

Organizations still caught in this archaic annual ritual need to ask themselves, is this truly the best way to provide feedback to our most important resource? Or is there a way we can do it with more frequency and meaning?

What these number systems do offer is a framework for corporations to implement merit pay systems, which adds yet another level of complexity into the mix. Then each manager is told, *Based on this year's profits, only 20 percent of your team can get an average of a 4, and so on.* Managers who do not want a performance review to result in an employee's less-than-expected salary increase will then artificially inflate the score. Now the performance review no longer meets the primary objective of reflecting their performance and offering honest feedback.

Inevitably, every person who has experienced a numeric ranking system has said the application of the numbers is subjective. You hear, *I never give 5s to anyone, no matter how good they are.* Each supervisor applies the numeric system to his or her own philosophy, even though the heart of the numeric system is to keep it objective and consistent across the organization. So

ORGANIZATIONS STILL CAUGHT IN THIS ARCHAIC ANNUAL RITUAL NEED TO ASK THEMSELVES, IS THIS TRULY THE BEST WAY TO PROVIDE FEEDBACK TO OUR MOST IMPORTANT RESOURCE?

if we've failed at that, let's just set the numbers aside and use our voices. Have a conversation with staff within a framework of what we really need to know about performance. Then type up a paragraph or two that captures the conversation and lays out measurable goals for moving forward. Done. Simple. Effective.

A survey of 1,149 workers at 79 different companies found that manager feedback and coaching skills were consistently rated as *mediocre.* If an employee's line of sight is unfettered and clear, then they want to know how they are doing in their individual contribution to the organization. Providing feedback isn't an event, it's a relationship. Remember, the number-one driver of engagement is an employee's relationship with their supervisor. These regular conversations go far beyond meeting the mandate of performance reviews. They feed and nourish the boss-employee relationship. They give the performance review process social-capital-building purpose.

After analyzing performance reviews, feedback surveys and nominations for management awards, Google found what employees valued most were *even-keeled bosses who made time for one-on-one meetings, helped them solve problems, and took an interest in their lives and careers.* As stated by London Business School's organizational behavior expert

Nigel Nicholson, "The manager needs to look at the employee not as a problem to be solved, but as a person to be understood."

In 2001 after the New York Yankee's fourth World Series victory in just five years, an article ran in Fortune magazine headlined, "A Manager for All Seasons: Joe Torre gets the most out of his workers, makes his boss happy, and delivers wins. He may be the model for today's corporate managers. And he's not afraid to cry." The Yankees hadn't won a World Series since 1981, and the article attributed the team's turn-around to Torre's unique management style of developing meaningful, trusting, empathetic and loyal relationships with each individual player. As a former major league player himself, Torre summarized his management style by stating, "I try to understand what motivates other people." The author of the article went on to say:

> Baseball legend Gene Mauch once said that it's easier for 25 players to understand one manager than for one manager to understand 25 players. Torre operates under the opposite premise. He sets a few basic rules (don't be late, no excessive facial hair, no loud music in the clubhouse), but that's it for across-the-board edicts. His principal management tool is not the big team meeting – he has little use for generic motivational talks – but regular one-on-one encounters with his players, which he uses to both monitor and regulate their psyches.

Instead of using management positions as a reward for all career paths, organizations need to promote those most capable of creating meaningful relationships with employees, like Torre.

> **PROVIDING FEEDBACK ISN'T AN EVENT, IT'S A RELATIONSHIP.**

This important point of the supervisor-employee relationship is often forgotten in restructuring or downsizing efforts where middle layers of management are either significantly reduced or eliminated altogether. When managers have too many direct reports, this critical element of time for employees is the first to fall to the wayside, and turnover and low engagement levels are the immediate byproduct.

Frequency and Meaning

The lesson here is that, with the generational diversity that now makes up our current workforce, there is value in challenging current performance review systems and taking a step back to evaluate whether or not they remain meaningful feedback mechanisms. When it comes to approach and frequency, employee engagement author Kevin Kruse offers a simple and straightforward analogy for all of us to consider:

> Do coaches of sports teams wait until the end of the season to give rating-scale feedback to their players? "Hey Lebron, I'm going to give you a 5 on your jump-shot, but only a 2 on moving the ball around."

Stefan Falk, an executive at Ericsson (a Swedish telecommunications company), offered his managers a framework of sitting down with employees one-on-one six times a year, often for as long as 90 minutes, to discuss their level of engagement and pursuit of mastery. The improvements in performance were enough that Ericsson began using it in offices around the world.

Don't forget to include an employee's commitment to community service and alignment with the company constitution as part of this ongoing conversation. After all, our overall goal is to transform workplaces into communities and employees into citizens.

Feedback as Recognition

In addition to the performance review process, feedback is a cornerstone component of employee recognition - demonstrating that employee recognition does not need to cost anything to an organization. According to Gallup, employees who do not feel adequately recognized are twice as likely to say they will leave their company in the next year. Recognition is also responsible for 10 to 20 percent differences in organizational productivity and revenue. For example, in one large health care organization, a difference of 10 percentage points in how employees rated recognition represented an average difference of 11 percent in how patients evaluated their experience. Research has shown that these linkages hold true across all industries.

Getting positive feedback from your supervisor can be equated to other similar triggers of dopamine in the brain, such as winning, experiencing good tastes and smells, or listening to music. And we know that as humans, our brains crave surges of dopamine because it gives us a feeling of enjoyment and satisfaction.

For these neurological reasons, in employee engagement surveys, Gallup measures whether or not recognition is present every seven days. Many executives feel annual award events or employee of the month programs adequately satisfy this leadership competency; however, it isn't enough. Gallup states, "All the evidence suggests that the employee brain is perpetually watchful and eager for reinforcing signals – particularly unexpected, spur-of-the-moment boosts."

When is the last time you paid your employee a compliment? Sometimes this makes leaders feel uncomfortable, worried it may come across as insincere; but there are subtle and easy ways to do this with your employees on a regular basis. Try starting a conversation with, *This is why your work is so important…*or ending a conversation by saying…*and that is why I am impressed with your work.*

BRINGING TOGETHER CORPORATION & COMMUNITY

Step 8 – Allow employees to have control (over their work *and* their lives).

If values of the organization are *both* teamwork and taking pride in one's work, an employee must be able to also take ownership of his or her work. Leaders must be careful that they do not unnecessarily create barriers toward the fulfillment of organizational values by sheer design. Based on the company's org chart, how many levels of approval are there? How many silos? What are the reporting relationships? Does everything have to go through the CFO because he/she controls the finances? Who has control over how the marketing dollars are spent? Hopefully it's the same group of people in the organization who are being held accountable for market-share growth.

Structure and Ownership

Too many times organizations develop their structure around divisions and departments, and not ownership and accountability. As the leader, you may be giving your teams full rights to the four T's; however, the organization's structure isn't. People and the way they make decisions do not always fit into neat little boxes. Try pulling things apart and then put them back together based on which employees are most invested in and accountable to the outcomes.

> TOO MANY TIMES ORGANIZATIONS DEVELOP THEIR STRUCTURE AROUND DIVISIONS AND DEPARTMENTS, AND NOT OWNERSHIP AND ACCOUNTABILITY.

One writer I worked with was telling me how she was taking the time to update her portfolio to ensure it included her most recent projects. After placing the items in her portfolio and thumbing through the work, it dawned on her, *This isn't my work*. Too many fingers had been in her pot. She was left feeling conflicted for a couple reasons. First, she questioned whether or not she could legitimately include these items as *her* writing samples; and second, she wasn't certain she even liked the work and felt it represented what she was truly capable of.

When employees no longer feel like they own their work they disengage, and well, no longer take ownership. Supervisors who create these environments often look back at the employee perplexed as to why they aren't watching the deadlines, following up when changes occur, responding to stakeholder inquires, etc. Well, it's because that individual no longer sees it as their project and no longer feels accountable for it.

It's critical to distill where discretion, decision making and ownership of action resides when leading large organizations and departments. Too many cooks in the kitchen might create a fabulous four-course meal, but also a significant amount of scaring from so many knives in employees' backs from the dual that took place before the meal was served. Many times when good employees begin to disengage, it's because they're just not up for the fight anymore.

Success Inside and Outside the Office

Flexible work schedules lay at the heart of autonomy. They allow employees to be there for their families when they need to be, and allow them to have a life outside of work. Employees shouldn't fear negative consequences when they are meeting their performance goals, but are away from the office. Former Best Buy employees Cali Ressler and Jody Thompson coined this approach as a *Results-only Work Environment (ROWE)*, and attribute company financial gains as a result of the deliberate human resource shift within the corporation. The authors say today's corporate America operates under a myth: *Time + physical presence = results.*

> **EMPLOYEES SHOULDN'T FEAR NEGATIVE CONSEQUENCES WHEN THEY ARE MEETING THEIR PERFORMANCE GOALS, BUT ARE AWAY FROM THE OFFICE.**

Ressler and Thompson say employees are most productive when they feel like they have control over their lives. For years, being able to control your work schedule has been off the table as an option. It doesn't have to be. Reward employees for innovation, results and outcomes, instead of hours logged and eight-to-five face time.

Smart phones, remote access and other technological advances should be leveraged as gifts that make it possible for us to have more flexibility. Corporate cultures must be careful that these gifts do not have the opposite effect, such as holding employees hostage to their jobs 24/7, contributing to isolation, or serving as tools that foster distrust. A 2012 survey of working adults showed that 80 percent continued to work after leaving the office and almost 70 percent can't go to bed without checking their email one last time. Thirty-eight percent even said they checked email at the dinner table.

Researchers from Indiana University suggest it's within an organization's best interests to ensure employees have balance and fulfillment in other aspects of their life. They contend, when it comes to organizational policy development, it's important to understand how policy influences employees' ability to openly and comfortably engage in multiple interests, especially the ability to pursue non-work activities. The study goes on to say that success in one area of a person's life can energize and enrich successes in other areas. Gallup has found the same, indicating employees who are thriving in their lives overall are more

EMPLOYEES WHO ARE THRIVING IN THEIR LIVES OVERALL ARE MORE THAN TWICE AS LIKELY TO BE ENGAGED IN THEIR JOBS.

than twice as likely to be engaged in their jobs compared to those who are struggling. Smart managers are those who create a work environment that is conducive to employees being equally successful inside and outside of the office.

As citizen-centered leaders, we have a responsibility to first, recognize when things are out of balance; and second, create curbs and gutters to ensure employees have access to the balance they need. The most effective way for us to do this is through auditing our own actions and then leading by example. If you are sending emails on a Saturday, your employees may also feel like they too should be working on the weekends. If you are consistently working long hours and missing supper with your family each night, your employees will quickly feel guilty for not following suit to the same work schedule. It makes me think of a county administrator I reported to who worked hard to instill a culture of balance. If I was still in my office at the end of the day when he left, invariably I knew - without doubt - I was going to hear him say, *Go home, Kathryn.*

Time: The Loyalty Test

American companies often make long hours a type of a loyalty test. Stanford management author, Jerry Pfeffer, compares corporate America to corporate Europe and points to the fact that European companies and economies are approximately equal to the United States when it comes to productivity and productivity growth. Looking back, GDP growth over 10 years leading up to 2003 was much the same, with the only difference being Europeans took some of their wealth in leisure, while the United States made a different choice.

If you do not work for a global organization, this issue may not be as front and center. A woman I once volunteered with works for a global software company where her European colleagues are afforded considerably more vacation time. One time she forwarded me an out-of-office email reply from her colleague in Sweden that simply stated, "I will be out of the office for the next four weeks enjoying summer holiday and will return all phone calls and emails upon my return. Sincerely, Josefin." This isn't the typical out-of-office reply that we're accustomed to seeing as Americans; however, it shines a spotlight on the stark contrast between the European culture and ours where you see very few American workers taking more than a week away from the office.

Speaking of emails, perhaps the most popular example of America's around-the-clock work culture was demonstrated by a global Kansas City-based company. This is what the CEO's email said:

> We are getting less than 40 hours of work from a large number of our K.C.-based EMPLOYEES. The parking lot is sparsely used at 8 a.m.; likewise at 5 p.m. As managers — you either do not know what your EMPLOYEES are doing; or you do not CARE. You have created expectations on the work effort which allowed this to happen inside [this company], creating a very unhealthy environment. In either case, you have a problem and you will fix it or I will replace you.

> NEVER in my career have I allowed a team which worked for me to think they had a 40-hour job. I have allowed YOU to create a culture which is permitting this. NO LONGER.

The CEO went on to list six potential punishments, including laying off 5 percent of the staff in Kansas City. "Hell will freeze over," he vowed, before he would dole out more employee benefits. The parking lot would be his yardstick of success, stating it should be "substantially full" at 7:30 a.m. and 6:30 p.m. on weekdays and half full on Saturdays. "You have two weeks," he said. "Tick, tock."

The email was intended for the company's 400 or so managers, but ended up getting leaked on Yahoo. Subsequently, the company's stock tumbled 22 percent in the next three days.

Conversely, analytics software giant SAS is an example of an organization that couldn't be more tuned into the social capital benefits of work-life balance. SAS employees and their families have free access to a large gymnasium with tennis and basketball courts, a weight room and a heated pool. Also offered to employees is an on-site health care clinic, staffed by physicians, nutritionists, physical therapists and psychologists – all free of charge. Deeply discounted child care is available, in addition to no-cost work-life counseling which helps employees manage everyday-life stresses. Employees are encouraged to use any of these benefits offered on their campus at any hour of the day. For example, you'll often see people using the gym long after the noon lunch hour.

Jim Goodnight, who has been the company's CEO for over three decades, holds firmly that workers instinctively and positively respond to an organization that routinely demonstrates that they matter and are individually valued. One could argue that absent

WORKERS INSTINCTIVELY AND POSITIVELY RESPOND TO AN ORGANIZATION THAT ROUTINELY DEMONSTRATES THAT THEY MATTER AND ARE INDIVIDUALLY VALUED.

these programs and benefits, Goodnight could pay his workforce more; however, he long ago figured out that perks are symbolic representations of how he and his company value their people. The holistic offering of benefits constantly reminds workers that they matter greatly to the success of the organization.

In addition to the on-site benefits already mentioned, Goodnight adopted a 35-hour workweek structure. One key reason was because the firm did not want employees doing programming while they were exhausted. SAS says, as a result of their overall workplace culture, their programs have fewer bugs and therefore need fewer people to find and correct programming mistakes; however, most of all, the end benefit to all of this is the happy customer. According to SAS CMO Jim Davis:

> While we say we have a 35-hour workweek, I don't know anybody who really works 35 hours. The reality is if you trust people, and you ask them to do something - and you treat them like a human being as opposed to a commodity where you try to squeeze something out - they're going to work all sorts of

> hours. But they're going to enjoy those hours
> as opposed to "slaving in the office."

In order to earn a spot in SAS' management ranks, much like Suvarov Island's Ioane, you must first demonstrate a strong desire to help and support others. The primary responsibility of SAS leaders is to facilitate the career success of other employees rather than their own.

The company experiences annual turnover in the range of 2-3 percent compared to an industry average of 22 percent. Dollars the firm would otherwise spend on headhunters, training and restoring lost productivity can instead go toward further enhancing the workplace experience of employees (Remember the $42 million cost of turnover number from Chapter 1?). SAS, based out of Cary, N.C., has had 37 consecutive years of record earnings, which totaled $2.8 billion in 2012.

PwC (Pricewaterhouse Coopers) and Hobby Lobby are also examples of organizations that have adopted policies with the purpose of creating guilt-free time away from work for employees. PwC has provided extended holidays in some form since 2003. To encourage a week-long break for employees over the December holiday season, PwC started a give two, get two program in 2012 where if employees used two days of PTO during the December holidays, two additional holidays would be added that same week. In 2013, to create an extended Fourth of July break, the firm announced an additional holiday on July 5. And despite weekends being a high-demand time for retailers, crafting giant Hobby Lobby, with 556 stores in 45 states, is closed on Sundays to ensure employees have time for worship and family.

Reality Check

Times have changed and having control over both life and work is important. Remember, we're living in a society now where almost half of the workforce is now made up of women. It takes dual-income households to raise families. If we begin to allow employees to have even just a little more sense of control over their lives, think of the health care savings corporations can realize through reduced stress.

Gallup found that employees who are engaged in their jobs are generally in better health and have healthier habits than employees who are not engaged. Engaged employees have lower incidences of chronic health problems, such as high blood pressure, high cholesterol, diabetes, obesity, diagnosed depression and heart attacks. They also eat healthier, exercise more frequently and consume more fruits and vegetables than their unengaged counterparts.

EMPLOYEES WHO ARE ENGAGED IN THEIR JOBS ARE GENERALLY IN BETTER HEALTH AND HAVE HEALTHIER HABITS THAN EMPLOYEES WHO ARE NOT ENGAGED.

The irony is, even as employees are expected to spend more time at work, they are expected more and more to keep their personal lives out of the workplace. Advancements in technology allow organizations to big brother their staff by monitoring personal emails, time spent online and phone calls made. When you arrive at work, all of your other responsibilities and obligations in life, including family and community, are to be set aside. This is unrealistic and frankly, impossible.

A RETURN TO SUVAROV

Today's rapidly changing global market presents perhaps some of the largest challenges for organizations in the contest for talent and pursuit of profits; however, achieving high social capital is the best competitive advantage an organization can have.

ACHIEVING HIGH SOCIAL CAPITAL IS THE BEST COMPETITIVE ADVANTAGE AN ORGANIZATION CAN HAVE.

Corporations that turn their workplaces into communities and employees into citizens can achieve:

1. Increased profitability.
2. Increased operational efficiencies resulting from compelling cultures, increased trust and reduced turnover.
3. Healthier employees.
4. Brand differentiation.
5. An organization where everyone inherently (and willingly) belongs to the Marketing Department.
6. Employees who are more engaged in their work, families and communities.
7. Satisfied and loyal customers.

Collectively America Can Change

With a record-high number of dual-household workers today, transforming our communities and improving our economy has its best chance through a new kind of corporate leadership. This isn't to say that by following the recommendations outlined in this book we'll look exactly the way we did in 1950 when we were the most engaged. That isn't realistic. The structure of community has changed. But what it does mean is that if organizational leaders revisit what makes a workplace a community, collectively America can change. Parents will have more time to be parents. Governments will have interested and less reliant constituents. Organizations will have invigorated and loyal employees. Corporations will become more productive and profitable.

> **IF YOU HAD TO CHOOSE BETWEEN 10 PERCENT MORE TEACHERS OR 10 PERCENT MORE PARENTS BEING INVOLVED IN THEIR KIDS' EDUCATION, THE LATTER IS A BETTER ROUTE TO EDUCATIONAL ACHIEVEMENT.**

Harvard Kennedy School of Government's Saguaro Seminar conveys the impact and power of social capital through some of these examples:

> Social capital is the best variable to successfully predict levels of tax compliance state by state.

> If you had to choose between 10 percent more cops on the beat or 10 percent more citizens

knowing their neighbors' first names, the latter is a better crime prevention strategy.

If you had to choose between 10 percent more teachers or 10 percent more parents being involved in their kids' education, the latter is a better route to educational achievement.

If you had to choose whether your child was born into a poor state or low social capital state, the low social capital state is worse for the child's outcomes, according to the Annie Casey Foundation's Kids Count Index (low birth weight babies, unwanted teen pregnancies, teenage drug use, etc.).

Joining and participating in one group cuts your odds of dying over the next year in half. Joining two groups cuts it by three-quarters.

Starting at the Top

Not enough emphasis can be placed on the fact that, in order to effectively transform and build social capital in the workplace, it must come from the top. Organizations and departments take on the behaviors and values of their leaders. Top officials must provide both the financial resources and leadership to facilitate a workplace transformation that values the principles of engagement and promotes increased social capital. This includes key organizational policy changes that manifest into budget reprioritization, a fresh look at employee benefits, and a shift in how marketing dollars are allocated. More dollars will be directed to engagement strategies. Or go ahead and label it *customer experience* on your operating budget. They are one in the same.

IN ORDER TO EFFECTIVELY TRANSFORM AND BUILD SOCIAL CAPITAL IN THE WORKPLACE, IT MUST COME FROM THE TOP.

Here is what citizen-centered leadership doesn't mean. It doesn't mean picking out just one or two of the core competencies and claiming a workforce revolution. For example, you can't say, *Hey, that line of sight stuff makes some sense. Let's start a company newsletter so we can do a better job of keeping everyone informed. Done.* That isn't an employee engagement strategy. That's a one-off tactic that will produce just one outcome for you – keeping people informed - which doesn't equate to a cultural transformation.

The tides are definitely turning and many executives are recognizing how corporate leadership must change.

"I believe wholeheartedly that a new form of capitalism is emerging. More stakeholders (customers, employees, shareholders, and the larger community) want their business to... have a purpose bigger than their product."
Mats Lederhausen, investor and former McDonald's executive

The United Way's Laura Bowman describes local United Way Board Member and Ridley, Inc. CEO Steve VanRoekel as "the trifecta of corporate engagement." This trifecta is time, talent and treasure. (Three more T's for you to take with you on your leadership pursuit!) Ridley, Inc. is one of the largest commercial animal health nutrition businesses in North America, serving customers in the United States and Canada. VanRoekel serves on his local United Way Board, and his organization has over 80 percent employee participation with giving to United Way. He is a community mentor to an elementary-school student and asked his staff (all of the staff, not just the executives) to be mentors too. Ridley, Inc. most recently gave a $100,000 lead gift to build a local children's museum, and as part of the deal Ridley, Inc. offered their employee experts to provide content expertise to the development of the farm exhibit area. Long term, Ridley employees will be allowed to volunteer work time at the museum. Employees do not leave VanRoekel's organization and they are profitable.

Start the Conversation

You may not agree with everything in this book, but if you are a CEO or executive, what would your employees say? If you are a non-profit leader, what would your donors say? If you are an elected official, what would your constituents say? Start the conversation and see where it goes. Here is a checklist of the work in front of you:

Core Competencies for Citizen-centered Leadership

1. Develop a corporate constitution.
2. Ensure the work of the organization serves a higher purpose.
3. Make the workplace a platform for civic engagement and education.
4. Create transparency and community gathering spaces.
5. Invest in first-line leaders.
6. Create and maintain a line of sight.
7. Ensure meaningful feedback mechanisms.
8. Allow employees to have control (over their work *and* their lives).

No matter what industry you are in, by focusing on these core competencies, the traditional benchmarks and goals that we're all accustomed to as leaders become easier to obtain. Citizen-centered leadership facilitates an environment that allows all businesses to thrive. It's an economic stimulus package that collectively will move our nation forward as more and more organizational leaders participate.

Corporate America can provide a new platform for citizens to stand on. One that moves beyond the mission statement by building social capital both inside and outside the walls of an organization. Suvarov Island is now just eight steps away for any organizational leader. Give it a try. See where it takes you, your organization, your community, our country.

NOTES

Introduction: Ties That Bind

1. ***Letters from the Lost Soul***. Bitchin, B. (2004). *Letters from the Lost Soul: A five-year voyage of discovery and adventure.* Dobbs Ferry, NY: Sheridan House, Inc., p. 40-42.

2. **2013 State of the Union Address, President Obama**. Obama, B. (2013). "2013 State of the Union Address." *Washington Post.* Retrieved June 22, 2013 at http://articles.washingtonpost.com/2013-02-12/politics/37059380_1_applause-task-free-enterprise/9

Chapter 1: Corporate & Community Engagement

1. **70 percent of Americans who go to work every day are not engaged in their job. The cost of actively disengaged workers to the U.S. is estimated at $450 to $550 billion annually.** Harter, J., O'Boyle, E. (2013) "State of the American Workplace: Employee engagement insights for US business leaders," Gallup, Inc., p. 4, 9. Retrieved on July 27, 2013 at http://www.gallup.com/strategicconsulting/163007/state-american-workplace.aspx

2. **Only 6 percent are highly engaged.** Maritz Market Research (2010). "Move mountains with motivated employees." Retrieved on August 23, 2010 at http://www.maritz.com/tlps/EmployeeEngagement.aspx?source=gaw_motivation

3. **Engagement levels in 2010 represented the largest decline in 15 years**. Towers Watson (2010). "Towers Watson 2010 Global Workforce Study." Retrieved on November 12, 2012 at http://www.towerswatson.com/global-workforce-study/

4. **Economic studies demonstrate that social capital makes workers more productive, firms more competitive, and nations more prosperous.** "Better Together" (2000, December). Saguaro Seminar on Civic Engagement in America at Harvard University's Kennedy School of Government. Retrieved on Aug. 26, 2009 at http://www.bettertogether.org/pdfs/FullReportText.pdf

5. **Companies with highly engaged employees experience 19.2 percent higher operating income, 17 percent higher operating margin, and 27.8 percent improvement in earnings per share. However, within companies with disengaged employees, employees are absent 3.5 more days per year, experience a decreased operating income of 32.7 percent and a 3.8 percent decline in net income, as well as**

an 11.2 percent decline in earnings per share. Kelleher, B. (2010, May). "Louder than words: 10 essential engagement steps that drive results." Presentation at Innovations in Organizational Performance Management Conference, May 19, 2010, Mankato, MN.

6. **Organizations with high levels of engagement continue to outperform the total stock market index and posted total shareholder returns 22 percent higher than average in 2010. Companies with low engagement had a total shareholder return 28 percent lower than average.** Aon Hewitt (2011). "Trends in Global Employee Engagement," p. 6. Retrieved on November 12, 2012 at http://www.aon. com/attachments/thought-leadership/Trends_ Global_Employee_Engagement_Final.pdf

7. **Employees most committed to their organizations put forth 57 percent more effort and were 87 percent less likely to leave their company than employees who considered themselves disengaged.** The Staff of the Corporate Executive Board (2010, August). "The Role of Employee Engagement in the Return to Growth," *Bloomberg Businessweek*. Retrieved on November 12, 2012 at http://www. businessweek.com/managing/content/aug2010/ ca20100813_586946.htm

8. **100 Best Companies to Work For voluntary turnover rates.** Bourne, K., Kickul, J., Lester, S.W., Wilson, F. (2009). "Embracing the whole individual: Advantages of a dual-centric perspective of work and life." *Business Horizons.* 52, p. 387-398.

9. **While 90 percent of leaders recognize employee engagement is still the most crucial factor when determining organizational success; 75 percent admitted they have no engagement plan or strategy in place.** The Staff of the Corporate Executive Board (2010, August). "The Role of Employee Engagement in the Return to Growth," *Bloomberg Businessweek.* Retrieved on November 12, 2012 at http://www.businessweek.com/managing/content/aug2010/ca20100813_586946.htm

10. **Robert Putnam and the benefits of social capital.** Putnam, R. (2000). *Bowling alone: The collapse and revival of American community.* New York, NY: Simon and Schuster, p. 34, 254, 283, 426-429.

11. **Harvard's *Bowling Alone* website.** Factoids retrieved on April 14, 2013 at http://www.hks.harvard.edu/saguaro/factoids.htm

12. **Peter Block.** Block, P. (2008). *Community: The structure of belonging.* San Francisco, CA: Berrett-Koehler Publishers, Inc., p. 1.

13. **The average American worker clocks up to 40 percent more hours during his life time than the average person in Germany, France or Italy.** Pfeffer, J. (2007). *What were they thinking? Unconventional wisdom about management.* Boston, MA: Harvard Business School Publishing, p. 69.

14. **In 2009, married middle-income parents worked the equivalent of an additional day a week (8.6 hours) as compared to 1979.** Economic Policy Institute (2012), "The State of Working America." Retrieved August 18, 2013 at http:// stateofworkingamerica.org/chart/swa-income-table-2-17-annual-hours-work-married/.

15. **A new generation.** Sladek, S. (2013). *The End of Membership as We Know It: Building the fortune-flipping, must-have association of the next century.* Washington, DC: ASAE.

16. **The workplace plays a dual social capital role – nurturing it in some ways, and draining it in others.** "Better Together" (2000, December). Saguaro Seminar on Civic Engagement in America at Harvard University's Kennedy School of Government. Retrieved on Aug. 26, 2009 at http://www.bettertogether.org/pdfs/ FullReportText.pdf

17. **Robert Sutton.** Sutton, R. I. (2010). *Good Boss, Bad Boss: How to be the best...and learn from the worst.* New York, NY: Business Plus, p. 20.

18. **The cost of losing an employee is estimated to be one-fifth of their annual salary.** Boushey, H., Glynn, S. (2012). "There are Significant Business Costs to Replacing Employees," Center for American Progress.

19. **When it comes to attracting, engaging, and retaining talent - the second-most important business challenge facing today's CEOs - the level of priority compared to other business investments is ranked at 44.** Kelleher, B. (2010, May). "Louder than words: 10 essential engagement steps that drive results." Presentation at Innovations in Organizational Performance Management Conference, May 19, 2010, Mankato, MN, referenced in a 2009 Towers Perrin Study.

Chapter 2: State of the Union

1. **Walmart and Reverend Jim Wallis.** Wallis, J. (2010). *Rediscovering Values: On wall street, main street, and your street.* New York, NY: Howard Books, p. 85-87.

2. **Economic Policy Institute.** Mishel, L., Sabadish, N. (May 2, 2012). "CEO pay and the top 1%:

How executive compensation and financial-sector pay have fueled income inequality," Economic Policy Institute. Retrieved on June 22, 2013 at http://www.epi.org/publication/ib331-ceo-pay-top-1-percent/

3. **Recent research indicates four out of five U.S. adults struggle with joblessness, near-poverty or reliance on welfare for at least parts of their lives.** Rank's analysis (2013, July) Oxford University Press, as reported by NPR at http://www.npr.org/templates/story/story.php?storyId=206331546

4. **From 1978–2011, CEO compensation grew more than 725 percent, substantially more than the stock market and remarkably more than worker compensation at a meager 5.7 percent. The CEO-to-worker compensation ratio in 2011 was 209.4-to-1 compared to 18.3-to-1 in 1965.** Mishel, L., Sabadish, N. (May 2, 2012). "CEO pay and the top 1%: How executive compensation and financial-sector pay have fueled income inequality," Economic Policy Institute. Retrieved on June 22, 2013 at http://www.epi.org/publication/ib331-ceo-pay-top-1-percent/

5. **Robert Reich**. Reich, R. (2013). *Aftershock: The next economy and America's future.* New York, NY: Vintage Books, p. 60-64.

6. **Literature has shown when CEOs are given significantly higher pay and power than their direct reports, these gaps are linked to lower company performance.** Carpenter, M.A., Sanders, W.G. (2002). "Top Management Team Compensation: The missing link between CEO pay and firm performance?" *Strategic Management Journal, 4, Vol. 23,* p. 367-375.

7. **Standard and Poors CEO pay data.** Kuntz, P. and Smith, E.B. (2013). "Top CEO Pay Ratios," *Bloomberg.* Retrieved on July 21, 2013 at http://go.bloomberg.com/multimedia/ceo-pay-ratio/

8. **Peter Drucker.** Kuntz, P., Smith, E.B. (2013). "Disclosed: The pay gap between CEOs and employees," *Businessweek.* Retrieved on July 21, 2013 at http://www.businessweek.com/articles/2013-05-02/disclosed-the-pay-gap-between-ceos-and-employees

9. ***Conscious Capitalism.*** Mackey, J., Sisodia, R. (2013). *Conscious Capitalism: Liberating the heroic spirit of business.* Boston, MA: Harvard Business Review Press, p. 93-95.

10. **R. Paul Herman.** Herman, R. (2010) *The HIP (Human Impact + Profit) Investor: Make bigger profits by building a better world.* Hoboken, NJ: John Wiley and Sons.

11. **Psychological studies on CEO-employee ratios.** Bowles, D., Cooper, G. (2012). *The High Engagement Work Culture.* London: Palgrave McMillan.

12. **Four unmet human needs identified when people leave organizations.** Branham, L. (2005). *The 7 Hidden Reasons Employees Leave,* New York, NY: AMACOM.

Chapter 3: Your Leadership Pursuit

1. **Leonard Abess and City National Bank of Florida.** CNN (2009, Feb. 25). "Banker in Obama speech recognized for his generosity." Retrieved on August 23, 2010 at http://www.cnn.com/2009/POLITICS/02/24/obama.guests/

2. **Bob's Red Mill.** (2010). Retrieved on August 19, 2010 at http://docs.bobsredmill.com/index2.php?option=com_docman&task=doc_view&gid=5225&Itemid=29

3. **Moonshots for Management.** Hamel, G. (2009). "Moon Shots for Management." *Harvard Business Review.* February, 2009.

4. **Reverend Jim Wallis.** Wallis, J. (2010). *Rediscovering Values: On wall street, main street, and your street.* New York, NY: Howard Books, p. 6, 8.

5. ***Conscious Capitalism***. Mackey, J., Sisodia, R. (2013). *Conscious Capitalism: Liberating the heroic spirit of business.* Boston, MA: Harvard Business Review Press, p. 177.

Chapter 4: Values & Ideological Clarity

1. **Robert Sutton.** Sutton, R.I. (2010) *Good Boss, Bad Boss: How to be the best...and learn from the worst.* New York, NY: Business Plus, p. 18.

2. **Horny Toad.** Retrieved on August 23, 2010 at http://www.hornytoad.com/toad/do-the-right-thing/mission.html

3. **Tony Hsieh and Zappos.** Hsieh, T. (2010). *Delivering Happiness: A path to profits, passion and purpose.* New York, NY: Business Plus, p. 155-159.

4. **General Electric.** "Letter to Share Owners," Retrieved on September 2, 2013 at http://www.ge.com/annual00/letter/page3.html

5. **United Parcel Service and Viant.** Cohen, D., Prusak, L. (2001). *In Good Company.* Boston, MA: Harvard Business School Press, p. 21 and 97.

6. **When Gallup surveyed a random sampling of 3,000 employees, less than half felt they knew what their company stood for and what made**

their company's brand different from competitors. Harter, J., O'Boyle, E. (2013) "State of the American Workplace: Employee engagement insights for US business leaders," Gallup, Inc., p. 56. Retrieved on July 27, 2013 at http://www.gallup.com/strategicconsulting/163007/state-american-workplace.aspx

7. **Crate and Barrel.** Tonello, M. (2011). "Making the Business Case for Corporate Philanthropy," The Harvard Law School Forum on Corporate Governance and Financial Regulation, p. 3. Retrieved on September 4, 2012 at http://blogs.law.harvard.edu/corpgov/2011/08/20/making-the-business-case-for-corporate-philanthropy/

8. **Committee Encouraging Corporate Philanthropy.** CECP (2012) "Business's Social Contract: Capturing the corporate philanthropy opportunity," based on research by McKinsey and Company. Retrieved on September 4, 2012 at www.corporatephilanthropy.org/research/thought-leadership/research-reports/businesss-social-contract.html

9. **Sustainable Value Creation and Pepsi.** CECP (2012) "Business at its Best: Driving Sustainable Value Creation Executive Summary." Retrieved on September 4, 2012 at http://www.corporatephilanthropy.org/pdfs/resources/Business_at_its_best.pdf

10. **Novo Nordisk.** I know this to be true of this organization from meeting with a Novo Nordisk manager and verifying the information on the organization's website at novonordisk.com.

11. **Rich Winter.** Winter, R. (March 14, 2013). "RST Diabetes Prevention breaks ground for Wellness Center," *Todd County Tribune.* Retrieved on May 28, 2013 at www.trib-news.com/news/145-rst-diabetes-prevention-breaks-ground-for-wellness-center

12. **Millennials.** Sladek, S. (2013, November). "Getting Gen Y to Buy." Presentation at South Dakota Advertising Federation, November 19, 2013, Sioux Falls, SD.

13. **Blake Mycoski and TOMS Shoes**. *The Inspired Economist* (2008, October 8). "Tom's shoes: Buy one, donate one." Retrieved on August 1, 2010 at http://inspiredeconomist.com/2008/10/08/toms-shoes-buy-one-donate-one/

14. **Starbucks.** Retrieved on November 20, 2013 at http://www.starbucks.com/responsibility/sourcing/coffee

15. **Rolex.** *PRLog* (2009, January 29). "Rolex: The Rolex Corporation sets an example for philanthropy worldwide." Retrieved on August 23,

2010 at http://www.prlog.org/10174421-rolex-the-rolex-corporation-sets-an-example-for-philanthropy-worldwide.html

16. **Company Men.** Company Men (2010). Written by John Wells, Produced by John Wells, Paula Weinstein and Claire Rudnick Polstein.

17. **John Seely Brown and Xerox Park.** Emery, S., Porras, J., Thompson, M. (2007). Success built to last: Creating a life that matters. *Rotman Magazine. Fall 2007*, p. 25-28.

18. ***Built to Last.*** Emery, S., Porras, J, Thompson, M. (2007). Success built to last: Creating a life that matters. *Rotman Magazine. Fall 2007*, p. 25-28.

19. **The Container Store, Patagonia, Google, Panera Bread, Southwest Airlines, Costco and REI.** Mackey, J., Sisodia, R. (2013). *Conscious Capitalism: Liberating the heroic spirit of business.* Boston, MA: Harvard Business Review Press, p. 177.

Chapter 5: Citizens at Work

1. **John McKnight and Peter Block.** Block, P. (2008). *Community: The structure of belonging.* San Francisco, CA: Berrett-Koehler Publishers, Inc., p. 14 and 90.

2. **List of top volunteer grant companies.** Double the Donation (2013). "Companies providing generous grants to nonprofits when employees volunteer." Retrieved on July 14, 2013 at http://doublethedonation.com/matching-grant-resources/list-volunteer-grant-companies/

3. **Volunteerism statistics.** Double the Donation (2013). "Matching Gift Statistics." Retrieved on July 14, 2013 at http://doublethedonation.com/matching-grant-resources/matching-gift-statistics/

4. **First Bethany Bank and Trust, Timberland, Brinks, Hasbro, Stride Rite, and Sony Music.** Saguaro Seminar on Civic Engagement in America at Harvard University's Kennedy School of Government. (2000, December). "Better Together," p. 39-40. Retrieved Aug. 26, 2009 from http://www.bettertogether.org/pdfs/Work.pdf

5. **James Austin.** Austin, J.E. (1997). "Harvard Business School Social Enterprise Series No. 2: Making business sense of community service, p. 4." Retrieved on August 23, 2010 at http://www.hbs.edu/socialenterprise/pdf/SE2MakingBusinessSense.pdf

6. **Effectiveness of corporate volunteer programs.** Cihlar, C. (2004). "The state of knowledge surrounding employee volunteering in the United States." Retrieved on August 23, 2010 at http://archive.pointsoflight.org/downloads/pdf/resources/research/StateOfKnowledge.pdf

7. **Red Brick Health and Sundog.** I know this to be true of these organizations from visiting their facilities, Red Brick Health in 2010, Sundog in 2012.

8. **Lars Kolind and Oticon.** Cohen, D., Prusak, L. (2001). *In Good Company.* Boston, MA: Harvard Business School Press, p. 87.

9. **Tom Vonhof and Lakeville Police Department.** I know this to be true from participating in a facility tour with Lakeville Police Chief Tom Vonhof on May 26, 2010.

10. **Kelby Krabbenhoft and Sanford Health.** I know this to be true from working at Sanford Health.

Chapter 6: Management Designed to Engage

1. **When Gallup conducted a survey of over 80,000 employees, it learned the number-one driver of engagement is an employee's relationship with**

their supervisor. A 2009 Sirota Intelligence Study also revealed that disengaged managers are three times more likely to have disengaged employees. Kelleher, B. (2010, May). "Louder than words: 10 essential engagement steps that drive results." Presentation at Innovations in Organizational Performance Management Conference, May 19, 2010, Mankato, MN.

2. **Henry Mintzberg**. Mintzberg, H. (2009). Rebuilding companies as communities. *Harvard Business Review*. July-August, 2009.

3. **Daniel Pink and *Drive*.** Pink, D. (2009). *Drive: The surprising truth about what really motivates us.* New York, NY: Penguin Group, p. 104-105, 111, 115.

4. **Bob Kelleher.** Kelleher, B. (2010). "Louder than words: 10 essential engagement steps that drive results." Presentation at Innovations in Organizational Performance Management Conference, May 19, 2010, Mankato, MN.

5. ***Conscious Capitalism.*** Mackey, J., Sisodia, R. (2013). *Conscious Capitalism: Liberating the heroic spirit of business.* Boston, MA: Harvard Business Review Press, p. 52.

6. **A recent multi-year study tracked day-to-day activities, emotions and motivational levels of**

hundreds of workers in a variety of workplace settings. Amabile, T.M., Kramer, S.J. (2010). "What really motivates workers: Understanding the power of progress." *Harvard Business Review,* January/February 2010.

7. A survey of 1,149 workers on manager feedback and coaching. Branham, L. (2005). *The 7 Hidden Reasons Employees Leave*, New York, NY: AMACOM.

8. Google and performance evaluations. Bryant, A. (March 12, 2011). "Google's Quest to Build a Better Boss." *New York Times.* Retrieved Sept. 1, 2012 at http://www.nytimes.com/2011/03/13/business/13hire.html?pagewanted=all&_r=0

9. Nigel Nicholson. Branham, L. (2005). *The 7 Hidden Reasons Employees Leave*, New York, NY: AMACOM.

10. Joe Torre. Useem, J. (April 30, 2001). "A Manager For All Seasons: Joe Torre gets the most out of his workers, makes his boss happy, and delivers wins. He may be the model for today's corporate managers. And he's not afraid to cry." *Fortune.* Retrieved September 3, 2013 at http://money.cnn.com/magazines/fortune/fortune_archive/2001/04/30/301967/index.htm

11. **Kevin Kruse.** Kruse, K. (July 9, 2012). "The Performance Appraisal: A Workplace Evil That Must Be Destroyed Like a Blood Sucking Vampire," *Forbes.* Retrieved on Nov. 14, 2012 at http://www.forbes.com/sites/kevinkruse/2012/07/09/performance-appraisal/

12. **Stefan Falk and Ericsson**. Pink, D. (2009). *Drive: The surprising truth about what really motivates us.* New York, NY: Penguin Group, p. 117.

13. **Feedback as recognition.** Harter, J., Wagner, R. (2007). "The Fourth Element of Great Managing: Employees may be motivated by many different things, but they all strive for a surge of dopamine," *The Gallup Management Journal Online*, August, 9, 2007.

Chapter 7: Bringing Together Corporation & Community

1. **Cali Ressler and Jody Thompson, Best Buy.** Ressler, C., Thompson, J. (2008). *Why Work Sucks.* New York, NY: Penguin Group, p. 13.

2. **A 2012 survey of working adults showed that 80 percent continued to work after leaving the office and almost 70 percent can't go to bed without checking their email one last time. Thirty-eight percent even said they**

checked email at the dinner table. Perez, S. (July 2, 2012). "80% of American Work 'After Hours,' Equaling an Extra Day of Work Per Week," *Techcrunch*. Retrieved on August 19, 2013 at http://techcrunch.come/2012/07/02/80-of-americans-work-after-hours-equaling-an-extra-day-of-work-per-week/.

3. **Researchers from Indiana University suggest it's within an organization's best interests to ensure their employees have balance and fulfillment in other aspects of their life.** Bourne, K., Kickul, J., Lester, S.W., Wilson, F. (2009). "Embracing the whole individual: Advantages of a dual-centric perspective of work and life." *Business Horizons. 52*, p. 387-398.

4. **Employees who are thriving in their lives overall are more than twice as likely to be engaged in their jobs compared to those who are struggling.** Harter, J., O'Boyle, E. (2013). "State of the American Workplace: Employee engagement insights for US business leaders," Gallup, Inc., p. 52. Retrieved on July 27, 2013 at http://www.gallup.com/strategicconsulting/163007/state-american-workplace.aspx

5. **Jerry Pfeffer.** Pfeffer, J. (2007). *What were they thinking? Unconventional wisdom about management.* Boston, MA: Harvard Business School Publishing, p. 69.

6. **CEO email.** Wong, E. (April 5, 2001). "A Stinging Office Memo Boomerangs; Chief Executive Is Criticized After Upbraiding Workers by E-Mail." *New York Times*. Retrieved on Nov. 14, 2012 at http://www.nytimes.com/2001/04/05/business/stinging-office-memo-boomerangs-chief-executive-criticized-after-upbraiding.html?ref=cernercorporation

7. **SAS.** Crowley, M. (2013). "How SAS Became the World's Best Place to Work." *Fast Company*. Retrieved on July 21, 2013 at http://www.fast-company.com/3004953/how-sas-became-worlds-best-place-work

8. **PwC (Price-Waterhouse Coopers).** I know this to be true from contacting PwC about their holiday policies.

9. **Hobby Lobby.** Hobby Lobby states on its posted hours that it is closed on Sundays to provide employees with time for family and worship.

10. **Employees who are engaged in their jobs are generally in better health and have healthier habits than employees who are not engaged.** Harter, J., O'Boyle, E. (2013). "State of the American Workplace: Employee engagement insights for US business leaders," Gallup, Inc.,

p. 50. Retrieved on July 27, 2013 at http://www. gallup.com/strategicconsulting/163007/state-american-workplace.aspx

Conclusion: A Return to Suvarov

1. **Saguaro Seminar Social Capital Factoids.** Factoids retrieved on April 14, 2013 at http:// www.hks.harvard.edu/saguaro/factoids.htm

2. **Mats Lederhausen, investor and former McDonald's executive.** Pink, D. (2009). *Drive: The surprising truth about what really motivates us.* New York, NY: Penguin Group, p. 134.

ABOUT THE AUTHOR

Kathryn Nermoe, who grew up in Iowa the daughter of an evangelical preacher and a music teacher, is an organizational-leader-turned-engagement-evangelist. With a background in government and health care, Nermoe has held executive leadership positions in the private, public and non-profit sectors. Her book focuses on a common and pervasive thread woven between all three: The need for engagement - employee engagement, citizen engagement and donor engagement.

Nermoe has never been one to embrace status quo. She sees the broad possibilities of both citizenship and organizational performance in today's rapidly changing economy; but only if leaders fully appreciate the impact social capital has on community and corporation. When organizations successfully engage their workforce, not only does it improve operational performance and profitability, it translates into an engaged society and stronger economy.

Throughout her 17-year career, she has helped organizations implement the steps provided as solutions in her book. She contends companies that have the broadest leadership support to implement all eight steps can truly transform their organizations, the lives of their employees, the communities they serve and even their customers.

In *I've got the mission statement, now what?* Nermoe integrates her personal experiences and a passion for organizational excellence with research.

Nermoe holds a bachelor's in public administration and public relations from Minnesota State University, Mankato; a master's in public administration from the Hamline University School of Business, St. Paul; and a mini-masters in health care administration from the University of St. Thomas, Minneapolis. She is a marketing advisor for Sanford Health, the nation's largest rural, non-profit health care system. She is married with two step daughters and considers Sioux Falls, SD, The Apostle Islands, WI and North Caicos, BWI all home.

Continue the conversation at facebook.com/Citizen Centered.